BNP

BEST NEW POETS

2022

50 Poems from Emerging Writers

Guest Editor Paula Bohince

Series Editor Jeb Livingood

This book is published in cooperation with *Meridian* (readmeridian.org)
and the University of Virginia Press (upress.virginia.edu).

For additional information, visit us at
bestnewpoets.org
twitter.com/BestNewPoets
facebook.com/BestNewPoets

Cover design by 4 Eyes Design, 4eyesdesign.com

Text set in Adobe Garamond Pro and Gill Sans

Printed by Lightning Source

ISBN: 978-0-9975623-6-1
ISSN: 1554-7019

Contents

About Best New Poets

Welcome to *Best New Poets 2022*, our eighteenth annual anthology of fifty poems from emerging writers. At *Best New Poets* we define "emerging writer" narrowly: our anthology only features poets who have not yet published a book-length collection of their own poetry. Our goal is to provide special encouragement and recognition to poets just starting in their careers, the many writing programs they attend, and the magazines that publish their work.

From February to May of 2022, *Best New Poets* accepted nominations from writing programs and magazines in the United States and Canada. Each program and magazine could nominate two writers, and those poets could send a free submission to the anthology. For a small entry fee, writers could also submit poems as part of our open competition. Eligible poems were either published after January 1, 2021, or unpublished. Which means you are not only reading new poets in this book, but also some of their most recent work.

In all, we received just under 2,000 submissions for a total of nearly 3,700 poems. A pool of readers and the series editor ranked these submissions, sending a few hundred selections to this year's guest editor, Paula Bohince, who chose the final fifty poems that appear here.

Sarah Ghazal Ali
Parable of Flies

I heard them, wings beating
a din beyond the thistle, pilgrims
beckoned by the promise of carrion.

Lured by the lurid, I followed
their song off the path, turned my back
to the lake. Angels fled the quarry,

thirst a blight in their wake. The flies,
their mouths roved like dogs
the breast of a sundered wren,

chest wide as a lens, steady
spectator of its own death.
This is an economy

of asylum. Ruddy flesh calls
come and brutes abound,
haloing their open-handed new home.

I'm divining my body a dirtied domestic.
When it rains, devotion is the womb
I've hollowed to keep desire dry.

Madeleine Mori

Tachistoscope

Watch for the target
symbol   the crossing
guard   the yellow
biplane   the red
baron   the black
widow   the rising
sun   the white
dog   the standing
man   the hostile
man   with a
cane   with a
duffel bag   crouched behind
the dumpster   who is wearing
a hoodie   who has
an average face   who has
no ID card   who needs
an immigration lawyer   who takes
ambien   who owns
the hostel   who runs
the hospital   who decides
the donor list   who delivers
the drugs   who makes
the teargas   who funds
the art museum   who disappeared
the relief fund   who wiped
the videotapes

See the man
who lacked   a mirror
who smoked   like a movie
whose costume   his self
whose ribcage   a xylophone
heartwood   justice
muzzle   oak leaves
who had mice for genitals
snakes for hunger
who lost   his hair
who lost   his guts
set his river on fire
but never jumped in

Benjamin Goldberg
Fugue with Allegory & Intake Room

A nurse skims plasma from your day-old wolf
tattoo. He sweeps the muzzle with latexed
fingers, jotting down undocumented scar
tissues. You won't find a safer place to sleep.
Behind the Sonic parking lot last week, your
beater's backseat felt reupholstered with tater
tots & razors, transfigured by your dose-
dream. When you stumbled down the gulch
beyond the dumpsters, you spent hours there
pretending snow was gauze. Tonight, each
room has a name. Day. Quiet. Authorized
Persons Only. Tonight, a boy beside you
sleeps so wildly, his sigh grows burning
hooves & gallops through cinderblock into
another blizzard. A pamphlet will explain:
your sickness is a statue. Your sickness is two
brothers, draped in stone & mounted above
two iron gates. The left, reclined. The right, in
chains. You spend hours flipping swords &
flowers into piles, reading bubbles scribbled
onto face cards. You contribute to the
conversation. Clothed & skin, you play
Lightning without laces. You're handed paper
cups & your blood greets angels by their
chemical names. From here, the view
constricts. A quarter-acre of clover field. High
beams on the muted interstate. Your ritual

before the doses win: list famous lunatics, call them kin, picture what they'd weave from what your eyes are given. Gardens blooming through each link of diamond-wire. A full night's sleep inside the floodlight. Between the window & its mesh, an emerald beetle will time-lapse into dust. Your task: the glassless mirrors don't believe you, & before you leave, they must.

Alixen Pham

The Burden of Translation

My mother carried an old man
on her back after she fled Vietnam.
He was small and shriveled, like a mummy,
limbs broken and reassembled
into a folded child.
He had a musky smell to him,
like river mud encrusted with broken houses.
She cried when she thought of him,
longed to see his black-framed glasses,
feel his nimble fingers whittle wood
into trees again.
But the authorities denied his visa, leaving
him to drown like a flooded ship, alone.
My mother built an altar to honor his bones,
the wisps of his hair, the psalms he used to sing to her.
She chewed bitterroot, ate dark shade
that had accumulated from centuries of oppression.
The Chinese, the French, the Americans, the Communists.
I didn't recall if she passed him onto me, or
if I took him on my back, or when it happened.
Only that I stitched a jacket for him
from the soft skin of my belly, cobbled his soles
on top of my feet, kept him red as I turned blue. Because
the river was where I'd come from. Because
the river curved wounds on my wrists.
I brought him to college, on first dates, draped
his sheets over them. I slaved my world for him,

wrote love poems, cried his name into the abyss.
But I nearly died beneath his weight. Left him
in the wilderness along with my thymus. After
my mother died, I realized I'd been carrying
the wrong person, calling him by the wrong name.

—Nominated by *Salmander*

Kuhu Joshi

Raag Desh

Where is the prince who will save me? Where?
I slept for a long time, tongue stale in my mouth.
My mother says *there are sweet boys, kind.*
I don't think she means my father.
But they will want things for my life, I say,
their mothers will make the fluffiest pooris,
add to the heap on my plate, dash to the kitchen for a spoon.
Mother, how will I refuse? I was made to please. All I know
is give, give. *Daughters will always*
blame their mothers, she says. I played the violin,
mamma, for years, because you said I must stick
to the instrument I chose. There was only one teacher
and I was his only student, practicing the drawl
of his favorite raag. I admit
I liked the raag. It was an evening raag, to be played in the rain,
in monsoon. He sat on the pedestal crossing his legs
and I sat underneath on the dank red carpet, moving the bow
with my wrist, elbows to the air. The room reeked
of rosin. He too, was a sweet man. Tender,
careful not to touch me when he could. *There is*
another path for you, my mother said. *Lonely, but honorable.*

Cai Rodrigues-Sherley

"It Took a Long Time"

from Nightbirds

In the static & blue
I showed a man my headless body
& for the moment I was
his twirling, private dancer—

collar bone & belly button,
shoulder, spinal cord, shoulder,
belly button & collar bone.

Someday soon I will know how it feels
to be touched by him & in the after
I will tell you the feeling, tell you
so you know.

//

At night I dream
of his hands smelling of lemons,
my skin shaved just the way
he likes, ready
to be reborn

beneath him, the press
of his instruments shaping
fell into flatland & all
the time humming
into my closed eyelids

a tune of my choosing,
because I am a power bottom
on his best tabletop & he does
what I tell him to & I tell him
to tear me apart.

//

Next weekend I am going
to see my mother
in her garden. I will not tell her
that I have been asking strangers to touch me
on the internet.
Begging them, offering
to pay for it myself.

Next weekend
I will visit my mother's garden,
 shed this old skin
into that familiar soil.
I will not tell her that I am going
to let a man permanently dissolve & extract
the majority of my breast tissue,
re-contour my chest & graph
new nipples. I will not tell her about
the potential loss of sensation.
the cost of transaction.
the song I want
whispered
in my ear.

//

On Friday, November 13th I will tell you
how it feels. I will tell you so you know
what to expect when you let
someone touch you
like this.

—Nominated by the New York University Creative Writing Program

Grace MacNair
Necessity Is the Mother of Invention

for Marie Anne Victoire Gillain Boivin (9 April 1773–16 May 1841)

That Necessity is a woman is no surprise,
but as one who mothers, I marvel: where did she find
the time between the washing, the nursing
of children, the dying—of the male ego, etc.

As one who mothers, I marvel: how did she find
herself again, widowed, her daughter dead—
and still the washing, the nursing at the charity hospital
for fallen women dying of what men gave them.

Herself, again, at the bedside of widows, daughters dead,
their babies still inside. A surgeon in practice but not name
because operating on fallen women dying of what men gave them
is simply taking care of others as women always do.

Their babies are still inside. A surgeon in practice but not name.
She had an eye at the tip of each finger, a fellow surgeon said
of her, Marie, a simple woman taking care of others as women always do.
Meanwhile, she invents the speculum, hears the fetal heart gallop for the first time.

She had an eye at the tip of each finger, a fellow surgeon said.
In all that time between the washing and the nursing,
Marie invented the speculum, heard the gallop she'd carry never again.
That Invention was stolen from her comes as no surprise.

Wyeth Thomas

The Heir of All Knowing Is Forgetting

I once dreamt that God
was a girl in a flour sack dress
rolling clay between Her tiny
fingers. She started easy making
snakes, fish, moonbeams,
the Ziggurat of Ur; graduated
quickly to mule deer, beargrass,
the Basílica de la Sagrada
Família; and wept at the beauty
of Her loveliest creations:
quasars, Yosemite, democracy,
Paul Newman. Five trillion years
later, lying in her great hammock,
thinking of all the old colors
and voices, She forgot
the word "molasses." It scratched
like wool at the tip of Her
enormous, old tongue. "Mollusk,
mollycoddle, moldering, molest?!"
It chafed at Her all afternoon
so that She could not enjoy
the way the eucalyptus trees
knuckled the darkening heavens
or the way the fog rolled in from
the bay, slow as…as…as…
She could not say.

—Nominated by the University of Utah Creative Writing Program

Willie Lee Kinard III
A Tangle of Gorgons

The lesbians that lived in the apartment to the left
of my grandmother's were always described in whispers.

    Caught in her teeth, her jokes: a pile of serpents
    thrown at her neighbors for stealing her appetite

        —always hurried, always hushed, hissing her "sissies"
        & "scissoring" as if the slurs would set them straight.

            It's a complex: to return callous to the same snake
            den reminding you of your own head's sibilance.

                I am of that ilk, I suppose: dreadful
                by happenstance, mere blinking having stopped

                    many a man in his tracks before me. Forbidden
                    to enjoy it, this calcified lineage.

                Like mighty Stheno & Sister Euryale, our family
                name insists wartime: those of us battling this curse

        of loving men never cease to stop making rocks
        of them, I, hating their waters, never able to skip any.

They don't make it that far. Somehow, always sinking,
always cracking, always losing parts of themselves.

Before my father's cleaving to fracture, I eroded
his visage to ruin. I barely recognize

him anymore, call him by his first name;
in my head, shortening the suffix. The second time

I cried for a man, my heart became a stone
I'm not sure I can pass off for a body part.

I don't often mention it, but I need
to speak on our history of numbness

—the golems we bear to know what it is
to bury a heart because someone abused it;

how I've seen it: every sorrow a reflection
I've avoided combing through, favoring the gleam

of being shorn bald. I must be specific:
I have mirrored these monsters before, severed

a personhood & expected it inconsequential.
But snakes won't stop coming out of my face now.

Their headless balm of displaced oil, preferring
the word serpentine to wolfish, litters

the sink with onyx scales graying as old money,
losing count of hours lost losing count

of bottles of Nair, losing count of quarters
lost promising men that they won't bite.

Unless unsettled, my mother bites, insisting my series
of settling unsettles her. I am getting upset again,

steaming at how I am always seen
as the unintended coven member, learned

in the ways the women folded their prayers
as they did their napkins—tucked in the center

of a lap in the center of a man in the center of a table
in the center of a lap in the center of a house

in the center of a lapse in the center of a judgment
asking why I'm still sitting inside, my uncles ponder.

The weatherworn heir, moistened of caches of secrets
of stoners & sisters of sinners in secrets in service

of sexes insistent on serving their bullshit
—I'm sure they too would prefer me headless.

It is frightening: I come from a stony people,
my own uncle's middle name meaning gem.

My grandma was clever like that, slipped regal
wishes into her children as if to imbue

them with crowns instead of petrifying them.
We are skilled in this type of sorcery,

tangling regret with dissatisfaction
when sulking a *sorry* might not be enough.

But, it slinks off our lips anyway,
disdain's silhouette appearing only in light

    of our gorgonry, this, our mother tongue,
    how we stilled our anguish, scarred our statues

        of psyches so, our countenances bled millennia
        before we ever turned to stone.

            Hear them whisper what my secret is:
            I have hardened for men many a day,

                wantoned my waist 'round unwanted Perseans
                just to see if I could still do it again.

            I wound. They whined. They slunk. They swung.
            They spat. They struck. They slung that weak shit

        like they just knew they were hitting it right
        —their ego, its scissor, a sword-swallowing cut

intent on making a trophy of me—I'm stunned.
My God. They never remember the head.

Ross White
Mule

Growing up in the South is like kicking a mule
>   to feel eternity in your bones.
>>   Or kicking a scarecrow, and calling it a mule.
Or running your fingers over the rusted,
>   abandoned blade from a tractor
>>   in its eternal rest, and calling that a mule.

You'll call anything a mule. Lace doilies
>   on the dining room table, the white-suited mayor
>>   leaning on a pearl-handled cane,
six loafy mutts chewing kibble beneath a carport,
>   call any of those a mule. Call the septic tank
>>   a mule, call the ATV and ammunition a mule.

You'll take a mile if someone gives you a mule.
>   You go to church every Sunday and pray
>>   to that ornery mule on his cross-shaped plow.
Summers, my cousins toss empties
>   from the F-150 as they drive by the high school
>>   and they call those empties mules.

They fly the flag their great-granddaddies died for
>   and they're proud of that ugly, bloodied old mule
>>   even though it stood for something they claim
it didn't and don't know why it offends so now.
>   Mercy's its own kind of mule but those cousins
>>   can't hear its voice too well.

I kick my mule sometimes and sometimes
        it rides me, climbs right up on my back
                and steers me to neighborhoods I don't recognize
in myself. My mule drags his plow
        through forty rocky acres I can't access.
                I promise, I'm trying to be a better person.

Arao Ameny

The Mothers

I read a news story about the mothers of
black sons and black daughters killed by police violence, how they gather and meet,
a network of four hundred mothers,
now son-less, now daughter-less,
how they call each other,
save each other's names
alongside the names of their children,
how they talk and cry and sing and laugh
and exchange photos and stories
to remember, to resurrect—

I wonder if the mothers of the police who killed them also meet
once a month, call, or cry or talk
about what their sons or daughters could have done differently—

do these mothers also meet and talk

about the loss our black mothers bear?

do they know
that they rest their hands on their wombs for days, sometimes for months,

do *these* mothers also plan weekends and holidays talking about what their own sons have done?

I wonder if they also get together on Sunday afternoons to drink lemonade, or sweet tea, to talk and cry
        and think and remember what life was like before any bullets left the gun.

Do they know that some mothers dream
of their children's faces, and these faces stuck in memory never age?

do these mothers of police officers also gather and meet? do they also have a network of mothers
whose sons and daughters have taken the lives of other people's children?

Again, I wake up to news stories about the mothers of black sons and daughters killed by police violence
how they gather and meet,
another day or night interrupted,

sweet air mixed with tears,
how they cup each other's chins and faces,

and pull in another woman as her shoulders shake, to mourn her child.

Still, still.

Madeleine Cravens
Creation Myth

Because a hand came out and pushed down the land.
Because a boy tried to hold two dogs together.
Because you wrote her about it. You sent a letter.
Because peacocks made cat-like sounds in the mountains,
and someone knocked twice, three times, on a smooth wooden door.
Because one's parents stared at each other on the delayed train,
gray commuters, and blood ran through a divot and bloomed,
became water spilling from the lion-mouthed fountain.
Because an impossibly large structure was built.
A pond used to exist at the edge of our city.
Mosquitos swarmed through the tall grasses.
Because one could die without knowing this,
the wild heart of all objects. In the dark, I mark myself:
One can be alive again. One can be alive ten thousand times.

—Nominated by *Raleigh Review*

Ashley Keyser

Eating the Siren

The ocean goes bluer as it warms and dies.
Phytoplankton carry off their green

to the poles, the forests gnawed away by urchins—
"roaches of the sea." But every creature on land

used to have a twin below, covered in scales.
Mermaids, of course, and more: a writhing haul

of mer-wolves, mer-rams branching horns,
a mer-elephant, which dwarfed the elephant

and gasped on the rocks when the tide pulled back.
Lions, too. The mermaids gave them suck.

Carved along church pews, they proffer teats,
while only Orthodox sirens have kept their wings

and vengeful looks like angels full of death.
Familiar hierarchies bound them, sea-bishops

ministering to schools of monkfish in habits.
East Indian mermaids lolloped in the sand.

They weighed some three hundred pounds,
slung with human breasts, which weren't enough

for the sailors to dream about, their nights torn
by some hunger too much to glut with a briny kiss.

Cooked merfolk, they said, tasted like veal.
The *sirenia,* on the other hand, tasted like beef,

Steller's sea-cow, like she and the siren
were slightly botched copies from terrestrial molds.

Unless the reverse were true, and they the prior,
more potent halves, the salt-glittery originals.

Lamps lit by their fat, those sea-cows are gone,
and the mermaid's tarnished girlish mirror

reflects dimly the moon she once held, her comb
demoted from a harp like a burning seraph's.

She might sing again, now that lions emerge
grimacing from permafrost with their fur still on,

the ice disgorging worms and Siberian unicorns.
Are they delicious? Pack dogs champed happily

on a wooly mammoth defrosting on a beach
at the beginning of the nineteenth century

in his waterlogged flesh and forty pounds of hair.
As fabulous beasts return, someone will find

a lucrative use for them. They must have flushed
with pride, the men who bagged the mammoth,

but they would truly rejoice if they knew
the Northwest Passage is at last melting open,

that route they coveted to spices, silk, its blue
a blue from beyond the sea, ultramarine,

for the robes of angels painted in our image.

—Nominated by *Copper Nickel*

Kōan Brink

Self-Portrait as Lake

If you drift,
if you drift further away,
if the lake drifts,
if the lake drifts further under
itself, if the drift turns
under itself, if I drift further
away from you, if I am capable
of drifting further away
from you, if the lake
decides to exit my body,
if the lake begins
to exit my body, if you
slowly exit my body, if
we exit in turns like dancers,
if the lake turns
slowly from blue to red,
if it slowly bleeds out
from our mutual body,
if the red bleeds into an open field,
if there is no water left
in the field, if there is no
safety in the open,
no trees to look forward to
with unblinking eyes,
if my life were just a film
by which I added
the occasioned dance,

if there was no real message
in the dance, if there was no
real human message, if humans
were no different than the lake,
if I had a feeling
in the end the pictures
they did not convey much,
the lake had nothing
to say, there was no particular
order to the pictures,
that in the end it takes a life
to drift and make order,
if I confessed
to having faith in the drift
itself and no particular
order, if I told you I believed
more in the going
than in the returning,
if I thought that people
don't always return
from the lake,
would you still return,
would there be
the possibility
of you returning, would
I have spent a life tasting
each thing
and eating nothing.

—Nominated by *Washington Square Review*

Kaleem Hawa

Haifa is a Punk Rocker

after Khalida Jarrar

In Haifa a storm front—
a front-facing eye of the storm,
a popular front
for storms needing
liberation from their skies!

In that storm front, a Haifa!
A Haifa where she got a phone call:

Hello, Haifa's mothers are on the line,
they wish to speak with you,
hope you're well,
hope you're sitting for this.

There was a time when a burial was an invitation
to congregate,
to bear arms, coffin bear,
bear palls,
for the Palestinians to allow themselves
to look at paper pictures,
and inscriptions,
and flowers,
and then pick up a brick
and throw it at a helmeted skull,
missing (you)
the target,
and chasing after (her)

the soldier to smash their face in,
and beating (them)
the eye sockets,
until they're mush.

The call came with a letter and the brick,
and a chisel and a green flag.

In my father's mother's memories of Haifa, in my mother's father's memories of Haifa, there are clouds! Suha, and Roula, and Yafa and Clara. They spoke it through the bars of the cell, and it tangled around the garden, wound through the street, and hitched a ride on the taxi cab, driven by the two Druze soldiers, smoking and petting each other in the dark, us in the backseat, drunk, they spoke it to us I swear, "This doesn't happen except in Palestine," but it does, storms everywhere there are mothers, and prisons too.

james mckenna
Long

Everything in the mirror, the world and me.

Things so far ahead I feel them tapping on my shoulder.

Harvesting basil, a call from my mother, my next shift, loneliness.

My mother tells me her only dream these days is of safety.

Another restaurant was robbed, have you called your aunt,

do not answer the door, they splash acid.

My mother has grown tired of dreaming. This country has hurt her.

Fear and dreaming and the world and my mother and the mirror.

These words fall as rain falls and land as what rain must become as it lands.

What I want is for my mother's life to begin, which translates roughly to dreaming.

A forgotten word for longing is 嫽, a woman standing next to a breeze.

For a long time I wanted every forgotten word because nothing else felt like this world.

When I talk about the world I often mean the distance between me and this mirror.

In my dreams of the mirror my mother is every word I have no meanings for,

meadowtreader, goldenrodshadow, 瞳眵年, *fullroomseason,* 龙争虎斗国.

Longing is the very edge of the world, where things move most.

Or, another way to say it is 想念, to remember the sensation of missing.

Or, 相今, seeing each other in this day, 心心, two hearts underneath, at the very bottom of things.

Justin Groppuso-Cook

How I Learned to Drink Oni, the Bitter Vine of Knowledge

By hissing icaros through cracking glass as butterfly
       bullets banged down Burlingame. By leaving the lights

on & doors unlocked. By holding sacrit space for no one
       there. By tin can phone & Wi-Fi—*Kano kano shamani*—

leaving voicemails to self. In the miração shaping umbra
       of celestial anatomies with melodies of metamorphosis.

By dieta, samá, in my sunroom embodying the silence
       of a Michigan winter. For hours that lasted unto the outer

reaches. For nights longer than my hair. By combing
       the desert of solitude like a Zen garden. By sinking into

the bitter cool of hardwood & unearthing solace. By shivers,
       quivering, sweats in the attic. By prayer candles the old

tenants left behind. By death, dead, dying: *O Santisima*
       Muerte! cradle me within your wings. By starlit vigils

& cicada hymns. By winds rattling trees, heat lightning
       seething. By milkweed & marigold. By the ashes, embers

of my mapacho. By shotgun shells, mason jars, an espresso
       cup or two. By taking the bullet in my dreams. The smoke

of mi pipa cauterizing the wound. By uplifting the name
       of my brother swamped in spirits—*O Jesse beautiful Jesse*—

as he breathed into sobriety: *Rami kano kanota, ocha nete*
       kanoya, sowa aketanara. By resurrecting the graveyard

shift. Yawning. By waking daybreak to drink a smoothie
       of abilla seeds I crushed beneath a knife—*Pisha pisha*

bainkin. By frigid showers, spasms, & spider webs. Purging
       the gossamer of piñón blanco, the rusted suds of sangre

de grado in my bathtub. By tingling with chiric sanango.
       By bobinsana leaves steeped in a cauldron of forgiveness.

By vapor baths—stovetop—of rose, toé leaves, mullein,
       ayahuma bark, & white cedar beneath a beach towel.

By the blood brain juice: piñón colorado, suelda con suelda,
       the greenest of apples—*Mucho! mucho!* boiled to moosh—

with a wink of limónes, honey to taste. Leaves of starfruit,
       avocado, & mango from E&L Supermercado. By water

fasting to tissue & bone around a thirty-gallon pot, waiting
       for that amber sheen to bubble & burst to the surface.

No more pork, marijuana—the guts of Honey Bourbon
       Backwoods on asphalt. Only plátanos, runny eggs, oats,

yams, & manoomin. A little adobo & Coca-Cola in celebration.
       Through revolt, revolution, a soft coup. By packages ripped

open, confiscated by U.S. Customs: *Bowie, may we see*
        beyond the cruel & unfair world. By yawning bygones.

Rapture. By *Noyarao joe kan*, palpitations & fluttering
        eyelids. By love letters sent into the flames. By breaking

up with myself, the past a dial tone. An oblation to everyone
        I've ever kissed—too much too soon I just couldn't wait—

Happy birthday to you. By Wilma & Enrique, the radiance
        of their coronas: parhelia across the canopy. By Merlita,

mi hermana; Wilder, mi hermano. By Hugo's motorbike
        & the little tributary in the Amazon where we drank, swam,

& sang: *Chiti chiti shamani, raro raro shamani.* By Matteo,
        my big bruv, & our layover in Lima: chain-smoking tipsy

in the glitz of nightclubs. By stretching sunrises in asanas
        with Michelle, her endless playlist of Drum&Bass. By alpaca,

cappuccino, & huachuma with Ross & Hamid. Miguel guiding
        us to mountaintop lagoons. By the chuchuhuasi, sananga,

& detoxes alchemized by David, his intentions sticking
        like condensation. By new kicks, ice cream cones, & cat

naps. Visions of my kitties intermingling with a jaguar.
        By backlight. By the self-portrait of Ole Grandpa Joe,

my mirror. By FaceTime with Daphne Metsá Noma, Victor—
        The Flying V—& sweet Toni, *O Tony Toné!* Conversations

cutting across vernacular & time zones. Our bladed tongues'
      luster: *Non jana rebonbi.* By the soft cloth of Celebrity

Car Wash cleaning & clearing the windshield. *Medicina*
      yonta ana. By Theodore James my baby nephew. By Lola,

Lily. The rest that are on their way. By bus. By Gratiot.
      Woodward. Calvert. Dexter. *By going where I have to go.*

Poetry of the Mumford Mustangs, Slum Village, Jay Dee
      on wax. Doing donuts down Hamilton in a totalled Lincoln,

no insurance. On the Lodge witit & back again. By Valerie,
      my long-lost grandmother, who paved her own mausoleum

from these schizophrenic streets. By sleeping with the Bible,
      Great-Grandma Nancy's rosary weaved through my fingers.

By tradition & translation, transmission & download. By bend-
      ing dimensions, physics, with the pitch & timbre of voices

not my own. By Yoda & Deany Deany Jelly Beany: *Bewa*
      bewa kakinra. By upholding the gravity of frequencies

my body was not designed to sustain. For I am the photons
      that escaped, waving away the event horizon. A shooter

of E&J & a single cerveza at seven a.m. to seal this energy.
      By my childhood home on Grove, my father's masterpiece

still evolving with flora & fauna in his passing. By the white
      hair of my mother's croning. By faith in the name I was gifted—

Sani Meni—& the gifts it brings to others. By delivery: *Neska*
    neska shamankin. By Groppuso. Martino. Degnore. Decaen.

DeMonaco. Cook. *Nocon shawan kaibobo.* All of this by *Noya-*
    rao torribo, Noyarao mi mujer. Yes, I am wed to a tree,

a flying tree. *Sí, todo esto de memoria. Y eso?* Her wings took hold
    of my throat resonating above the hum of streetlights.

Jacob Anthony Ramírez
The Lives of Jazz Fathers

Let's resurrect the trumpet players;
      the saxophonists named for fauna gone
extinct in the Congos and barrios,
      the worship and wail, the shadow song

of 40s noir—black and white ailments
      of New York's terminally cool.
There are no more quartets—
      only quartered ensemble split from

cities coated to chin, faces blurred white
      in pedestrian winds and yellow cabs.
Now, the drummers search estate sales, rummage
      for swivel stools to post on Etsy. The bassists

study phlebotomy, read blood panels for diabetes.
      The pianists work dental offices, drill tartars
to reveal the whites of cuspids. The saxophonists
      teach tai chi classes, sleep at the Chinatown Y.

I mean to say I miss them: the notes who stroll
      October for pick up chess in parks
with coffees and fingerless gloves; the chop
      chords at brick-and-mortar steak houses;

the soloists smile in the amber memory
       of nightclubs numb with intoxication.
They're dead—the blue veranda is silent
       where they jammed, moon drift in palm
leaves and ivory; notes of copper and zinc.

Gaia Rajan
I Tried Everything

Noise. And spite, and rock, bleach, black keys
on the wrong beats, wrong chords, coward I was,
inexact with my violences, writing quietly on buses
until the memory changed. I stood at the hinges
of conversation, not speaking except to agree
or repeat my name, staring at strangers' perfect
knuckles. I cradled a pigeon
and dropped it into my bed. I cracked open
a glowstick and drank what was inside. This looks
like a movie, I thought. It was nothing like a movie.
Fluorescent and sour. The flowers died
in my absence. I rented a beater and drove
until the rubber bounced off a nail.
This feels like a prison, someone said in a movie.
Nothing is like a prison.
When I looked up a Chuck E. Cheese had risen outside.
Neon smog, new mulch. I don't know
if this is a memory, but I remember it:
I staggered in the corridor past shuddering horses,
past strobe lights and wasps smashing out
at those improbable green, dead wasps on the tile
the windows the plastic flowers their bodies their bodies their
bodies I ran until I ran into myself until I

Brandon Thurman

New Moon Ceremony

What the hell is the big deal
about the moon? The poets
won't shut up about it. Even
my husband has started
stepping out into the dark
on the new moon with a bottle
of red wine & one of the prayer books
he bought off Amazon. I really don't
get it. *New moon* always sounded so
hopeful to me, but when I go
out with him, the sky is black,
I mean *black*, & the prayers sound the same
whether he reads from the little pagan
paperback or his hefty Jewish tome.
I suppose that should make me feel
good, one with all humanity or some such,
but all I wanted at that exact moment
was to go back inside. I mean, this is all so
human, right, to try to ignore the celestial
body that's up there throwing around
its gravitational weight like some kind of
god? In Hawaii with my wife—I know,
I know, what did I just say about
ignoring bodies, gravitational pulls—
she was bleeding again like she did
every month we failed in our duty *to be*
fruitful and multiply. Down on the beach,

we tried not to notice how the horizon
never seemed to end. What freaks me out
is how the wave that cracked my body
against that ocean floor wasn't even
that big. It was one of those moments
where your face is shoved into
the fact that you could just die, easy
peasy. In the residential unit
where I worked in those days,
the kids really did go crazy
on the full moon, though I tried
to write this off as *superstition*
or *confirmation bias*. It was like
they hid moon phase calendars
under their mattresses. This one kid
came at me with a literal metal rod
he'd wrenched off his bedframe.
After the kids finally twitched off
to sleep, someone would always quip
how it must have been a bloodbath
at the local ER. While we wrote up
our reports, Metal Rod Kid was only
feet away, shaking through sleep
under his Virgin Mother blanket
that stunk of night terror piss.
I confess. On the drive home,
I didn't look up into the sky
once. Back in the apartment,
I navigated to the bedroom
without flipping a single light on.
I slipped quietly into bed beside
my snoring wife. I still prayed

back then, so I probably did.
It would be dishonest of me
to describe here, at the end
of this poem, how the moon
was shining outside our window
while I lay in the dark counting shadows.
I'm not kidding. I really didn't look.

Maria Gray
Where Were You When Mac Miller Died

Instead of fucking her to pieces, why don't you
call shotgun in my Chevy. We'll whip around the rainy city
and I'll let you pick the music.
What's new? The talking heads on CNN say
it's gonna be a long winter. I say the winter never ends
and they don't know what it looks like.
Me, I'm spending the season holed up
in my childhood bedroom. Every night the temperature drops
and planets shift like plates across the sky.
Me, I'm waiting for Frank Ocean to return. Me, I'm
thinking of you, you jerk, never not
thinking of you and your not-new girlfriend,
your not-new girlfriend with blunt bangs
and blue hair, the vanilla genderfuck of queer love
between white kids in Chicago.
We have a lot to catch up on. Where were you
when Mac Miller died?
Has your mother given up?
Are you a real boy now? These are things I think of
when I'm not thinking of the virus. It's been years
and still your face is a ceramic plate
set at the table of my terror. After the rape I bled
like Mary. Like Eagle Creek I burned
and burned. And still when I got home
I pulled back the curtain to find you, in the shower,
wearing my clothes.

J. Bruce Fuller
They Said

they said beau was on that crystal and that's why he lost so much weight
come back from summer break looking long and thin
so the coaches moved him from left tackle to outside linebacker

and i was so skinny that kids made jokes and threw food at me in the cafeteria
they said eat a cheeseburger couillon they said

and i didn't want to be skinny no more and i didn't want to be weak no more
and i didn't want to do crystal even though beau was popular now
even though his new girlfriend was a real dixie queen
and when the ark-la-miss news said he was dead
i didn't understand and i didn't know they also called it meth

*

they said the lord wasn't gonna flood the world no more
but he must have forgot about us so we took what we could
from the waterlogged houses mostly guns mostly pill bottles
mostly things we could sell no questions asked

in my neighbor's house i smashed the door of a gun cabinet
and the deer etched on the glass scattered

they said take that shit hurry the fuck up
but i just stood there looking til we left
they said you a pussy you coulda made a fortune

they said édouard got sent to angola
and come back with a swastika on his neck

*

they said blood is made in the bones but oil comes from the gulf
and when the storms rock the rigs the chaplain takes confessions
and the boys cross themselves all night

they said big dan got blown up and burned all over
and now he lights his cigarettes with his ring finger
they said the settlement money is long gone

they said when the rigs catch fire some boys jump
they said them boys burn and even the water can't put them out

*

they said his daddy's a sonofabitch and they said he's a drunk
and they said he ain't got no daddy noways

i try to remember everything i don't know about myself
like is he inside here somewhere just waiting to lash out of me

they said you look so much like your daddy
you so much like him i could spit

and they said he killed a man and that's why he run off
and i remember the night and the kitchen sink and maman yelling
and the blood running down his face and i know it's true

*

they said if you don't fight him then we'll beat your ass
so i took the three-foot branch of pine
from the side of the road and i bashed his fucking face in

i can't remember his name but i know they say it sometimes
when they're drunk and looking back and thinking about how good they had it
back then when we were hungry and terrible and young

they said you one of us now they said you don't never have to be alone now
they said you did good they said you did good they said you did good

—Nominated by *The Southern Review*

Amy M. Alvarez
Hadeology

Gravity is the weakest force,
but it can bring a body down.

An adjunct professor on concrete outside of a church
A hood entrepreneur on concrete outside a three-story walk up
A schizophrenic son on concrete outside of his mother's apartment

A recent high school grad on a bathroom floor
A biking single mother and an eighteen-wheeler
A college student and his father's gun

Trillium
Cornflower
Aster
Honeysuckle
Poinsettia
Wild cane

We are electrons bound by nuclear pull,
magnetism. We spin out of orbit
and are pulled back a thousand times a day.

I only learned today what makes a glass
of water grow stale overnight. The obvious:
dissolved gasses. The strange:
the presence of geosmin—
molecule that scents earth after rain.

As the former outermost planet,
Pluto once had my complete affection,
but things change. Casey Goodson Jr.
did not get to inspect his newly cleansed
smile upon returning home. A good son,
he carried a bag of sandwiches home.

Last year, a woman I know taught
me a Turkish recipe for the purslane
growing wild in my front yard. This
year, the purslane did not return.
Instead, another woman told me
to make tea from the rosemary
growing rampant. Because something
always springs back. Gravity is fickle after all.

Cyndie Randall

J

At the funeral home, a man wearing a belt sees me walking
toward him on the beltwalk. He holds the double belts open
for me. Inside, I bring my soaking wet belt down from
over my head and shake the rain off. I sign the guest
belt, smell a bouquet of red belts nearby, think of you
fishing in our motor-less belt, your first new belt hanging
over the edge, hook waiting. Now, I see your face from where
I'm standing, still as the round pale belt in the night sky. I go
to you. I don't ask my questions. Sweet boy, unbuckle time!
Open your belts and see how we hold your mother, how we
wipe the belts from her face. Someone is strumming a belt.
Someone is preaching a sermon, licking his cracked belts
with a dry tongue. I want to take you home. I want you to say
what's for dinner? I imagine opening your door. The ceiling
belt is not bent and the room is not empty. There is no
leather belt coiled on your bed.

Kent Leatham

Blueprint

> *Purging the trope of the closet does not magically neutralize the external prejudice that the closet was erected to deflect*
> —Tom Joudrey, "The Troubling Resilience of the Queer Closet," 2019

> *Unceasingly the essence of things is taking shape*
> —Louis Sullivan, "The Tall Office Building Artistically Considered," 1896

Was the house built with closets in mind?
Is the closet an extension or afterthought of the house?
Is the closet an integral element of support?
Will the house collapse without the closet?
Can you price the house by the quantity and/or quality of its closets?
Is a house without closets a saleable commodity?
What does the closet say about storage?
What does the closet say about possession?
Does the closet believe out-of-sight, out-of-mind?
Does the closet intrude on or withdraw from the room?
Does it take up space? Is space freely given?
Is it a walk-in closet? Or can you only reach in so far and not more
to draw wanted items and articles out?
When they turn out the lights and close the door,
do the closet's contents go away?
What if it's a closet-within-a-closet, matryoshka-style?
Is it a straight house with a queer closet?
Does opening the closet queer the house?
Does emptying the closet queer the house?
Why did they build it if not to be filled?
Where else do you hide things?
Where else do you hang things?
Where else do you put things in boxes, in darkness?

Do we still punish children by shutting them in?
When they come out, are they properly reformed, rehabilitated?
Do we still hide there till the monsters are gone?
Are monsters still willing to claim that space?
Does entering the closet queer the monster?
Is the survivor that emerges the monster's mask?
If you pass a closet, does the closet pass?
Is the closet an archaic form and/or antiquated function?
Do we now prefer compartmentalized drawers
in matching bureaus and dressers instead?
Is the closet a functional part of today's holistic room?
Is the house old? Was the room repurposed from some prior use?
Is that why it has no built-in closets?
Is a china hutch a suitable closet? A dumbwaiter? A crawlspace?
How about a fireplace, furnace, or stove?
What if you make the closet a home in itself?
A micro-apartment? A rent-saving space?
What if the rest of the house becomes peripheral, disposable?
If you never leave, does the closet become a carceral or a monastic cell?
Could it be biological? Is it cancerous? Can it reproduce?
Is the closet well-built? Is there insulation?
Can stray nails snag an arm or scalp?
Is there carpeting down to soak up the blood?
Does the lightbulb with its chain of loose brass vertebrae still work?
Which side of the door is the handle on?
Is there a door? A beaded curtain? A porous openness?
Is there must or mold? Mothballs? Cedar chips?
A mousetrap or a roach motel?
Was the forgotten mink in the back ever real, or the peacock, or the calf?
Can they still be ethically worn, restored, reclaimed?
Are there photo albums on a dusty shelf? Love letters?
A single dried orchid or butterfly wing in a locked diary without a key?

Are there old board games?
Is there a gun?

The closet is for clean things, washed and pressed.
The closet is for hide-and-seek.
The closet is for storage.
The closet is for keep.
The closet is passive.
The closet, crouched and tensed, waits.
The closet is a knife block.
The closet is an attic, a cellar, a shed.
The closet is an outhouse, rank and thick with hornets and flies.
The closet has a race problem.
The closet is killed every day of the week.
The closet has been torn down, burned out, rebuilt.
The closet is a greenhouse.
The closet is a sunporch.
The closet is a school desk, a palimpsest carved with cocks and hearts.
The closet sits alone in a field.
The closet stands in the middle of traffic.
The closet has its own terms.
The closet is a vanishing act.
The closet is a two-way mirror.
The closet is a four-way stop.
The closet is a safe space.
The closet is an oubliette.
The closet is tongue-tied by a small pink triangle of flesh.
The closet is from out-of-state.
The closet is a bottle of pills.
The closet is a fountain pen.
The closet is a marriage guide.
The closet is a reality show.

The closet is a username.
The closet is your Gay Friend.
The closet is bearded.
The closet is bound.
The closet tucks.
The closet wigs.
The closet is apportioned.
The closet is appropriated.
The closet waits for a new law.
The closet needs quite badly to pee.
The closet has a UTI.
The closet has an STD.
The closet has to call the police.
The closet cannot call the police.
The closet hears the neighbors fuck.
The closet hears the bullets load.
The closet watches the enlistment commercial
while reading Code § 925: Title 10:
Section 839(a): Article 125.
The closet runs out of water in the desert.
The closet is sent back to where it will die.
The closet joins a caravan.
The closet scrubs its logos off.
The closet gets another tattoo.
The closet hides another scar.
The closet pours a cup of tea, mixes a cocktail,
sucks a fag to lower its voice, knowing cancer won't have time
to likely be the cause of death.
The closet sews another flag.
The closet turns another trick.
The closet works.
The closet votes.

The closet puts its heels on.
The closet straps its boots up.
The closet paints its nails black.
The closet puts its armband on.
The closet has a laundry list.
The closet has a hanky code.
The closet has a hawthorn broom.
The closet has a green carnation,
a blue feather, a unicorn.
The closet has its own app.
The closet was not approved for surgery.
The closet cannot donate blood.
The closet has no next of kin.
The closet has a dead name.
The closet has a candle lit.
The closet will never be "preferred."
The closet will never be "a phase."
The closet is refracted light.
The closet is a grave womb.

How long were you there?
When were you born?
Did you come out looking exactly like this?
Did you leave the door unlocked, propped?
How will you undress your next home?

Peter LaBerge
Sight of Love

Lake Chabot, San Francisco, 2019

Across the surface, the men of this coast—

    the lakebirds, grey reflections
skimming east

    across the lake. At the edge
of three years

    I hold Scott's hand, our reflections
floating to the bottom—

    pennies, floating like boyish desire,
milkweed-pink & faceless

    with rust, as I hold the memory
of tearing open

    envelope after envelope, of asking
the hotline specialist, *how treatable*

    is it? For a while, a BART train dangles
an evening call from a bridge. We talk

    as stars needle the lake
all over, as gulls

    swim into the lakefist & pennies
swim to a place where even light

struggles with breath, where we pretend
the man who had it didn't give it to me, didn't

crack my year open and watch it molt—
where I'm not afraid to check for the sight

of blood, where I can look at us—buoyant
in the night-gray lake, head on my shoulder, palm

on my chest, name in my mouth.

Fay Dillof
Little Infinites

1.
Remember *The Twilight Zone* episode
in which a couple tries to escape town on a train
that loops them back to the same station?

Like that, there are tracks in my brain.

2.
Halted on the highway,
my friend Amy says *We're not in traffic,*
we are traffic.

3.
I try not to look at the man in the park, doing pull-ups
on the limb of a tree. Sweaty,
bare-chested—he's always there.

Not that it's always the same guy.
Or the same poor tree.

4.
My father's cousin, when he still could speak,
asked *How big is your now?*
but I was already looking back on the moment

from some sad future.

5.
The gratitude journal I keep by my bed is empty
because every night it's the same:
trees.

6.
In the final reveal, the couple is trapped
in an endless game
being played by a giant child.

7.
*Well, at least she never stopped
trying*, my gravestone might read.

8.
When I say *soul*,
I mean like a photobooth photo—
quick this, this, this, oh, this.

—Nominated by *The Gettysburg Review*

Claressinka Anderson

Epigraph

> *The worth of that is that which it contains,*
> *And that is this, and this with thee remains.*
> —William Shakespeare, Sonnet 74

In the safe, something from years ago, never seen:
a xeroxed piece of paper with your handwriting.
A dream of sorts. Bewitchingly rendered.
You titled it "My Bridge." The night before you died,

I handed you the book with my poem in it.
You were almost done reading the complete works
of Shakespeare. Only a few sonnets left. Everything
underlined. Annotated. Left-handed, you were forced

into a life led by the wrong hand. Did you call me selfish
because I allowed myself a self? I'm a cliché, *Daddy*—
but you never read Plath. You came to me after,
in the kitchen, the light waiting on your forehead.

I read your poem, you said. Closed the book,
placed it on the marble counter.

Steven Espada Dawson

Elegy for the Four Chambers of My Brother's Heart

i.

We're under the same moon and I'm sick
      with that knowing. I want to peel it away
like a bumper sticker. Thumbtack Jupiter

      to this storm-angry sky. Jupiter:
Wellbutrin pill tucked behind that dark cloud's
      cauliflower ear. I listen for your name

in all this thunder. Shadows of buildings
      sieve moonlight like a family quilt. The city
empties itself tonight. Lightning stages this perfect

      vacancy like so many camera flashes.
For a moment, you are famous. Even god
      is looking for you.

ii.

The sugarcanes we chewed grew
from runoff water by the Tylenol factory.
Our daily hunt and gather, first stash
behind mom's back. We jammed them
between our molars and cheeks
like tobacco, found wild strawberries

big as a boxer's fist. You taught me how
to pitch rocks at the rainwater
pond. The slickest stones went farthest.
That was always the goal, right? To revolve
their bodies away from our own.

iii.

To wake me up, you'd press
my tongue to the nipple

of a AA battery. I press
my ear to the door

of AA meetings. Was that
your laugh I heard?

I'd try anything
to be better than you.

Brother, give me your turmeric
chews, your sexual awakenings,

your coupons for muscle
building milkshakes, your first

kiss. Give me your vouchers
for one free therapy session.

Shake out your boombox, please.
Press those D cells to my lips.

iv.

You're in a small room cutting
rugs. There's no music playing, no ballad
troubling your movement. Your bony legs
cross each other like witching rods.
When you shimmy the mirrors blush.
You've never looked so alive, down
lit through the skylight. The stars
are pinholes hemorrhaging moonlight
through a bedsheet. In the dream,
you sashay to the wall of my mind,
waltz through so many handfuls
of silence. You look gorgeous, spinning
the minute hand of a clock—forwards
or backwards, I can't tell.

Kinsale Drake

Blacklist Me

for Buffy Sainte-Marie

none of my ancestors are on the radio
none of my ancestors are
but my sister refurbished
an 8-track and I want buffy in her

purest form: NDNs huddled in a basement
somewhere, listening to bootlegged
tapes, except the basement's
not a basement. it's a truck bed—

(someone's uncle's GMC) wheedling
over a lip of river cuz
the best thing about rock n roll is
you don't have to do anything right

to survive. you don't even have
to make sense to a white english
professor who wants chronology
when I want buffy and a truck careening

into the horizon. I want the explosion
as grand as cicadas amping
out the sound of night as the 8-track
rolls and rolls and buffy

lives forever instead of on
some balding president's blacklist,
and through the smoke I almost want
to mistake a splinter of moonlight

for her yellow dress, all the NDNs
dusting themselves off
and laughing at the smolder,
the little wheel spin and spin
the little wheel spin

Sara Elkamel
In This Town We Rescue Cats

for Karim Ennarah

Amid November's raid, the journalists at the office
learned to make paper boats to pass the time.

Suddenly there were as many boats as people,
except not one boat had a name.

It is November again.

The boats collect dust
in the corner of the newsroom.

We sip coffee, sniff each whiskered abscess
on the lips of our strays

as officers question the salted lines
around Karim's eyes.

In our quest for temporary exits
we name strays; we make homes

in our terrible freedom,
which blinks, which

mortifies us.

To pass the time, we strain questions
like water through a round

mesh riddle.

Here, anything can be an editorial question.

Like can a piece of paper, however quaintly
folded, be a lifeboat?

Who takes a man,
post-swim, from the Red Sea,

who takes care of his strays?

We sip coffee, wipe peppercorns of grime
off the lips of our languid,

useless boats.

November again. The future
is a cold room with a bare bed frame.

Mariya Zilberman

Yanka Kupala Street

Family of metalsmiths who roofed
               this new city: I looked for our name
       in the cemetery. Found great grandmother in lime

next to a wasp nest. Envelope full of matte faces
               and a weathered map: I laid stones
       all over. Laid them in doubles

for the years none were laid. In the cemetery: found
               great grandmother in lime next to
       a wasp nest. Slaughter marker across from McDonalds.

DoubleTree near the mass grave. Placed stones
               in doubles for the years
       none were laid. At the river's edge, a flock of geese

cleaned their summer-plumped bodies. Slaughter marker
               across from McDonalds and DoubleTree
       near the mass grave. Green tufting

out of the bonerock, every city grown from
               the dead. At the river's edge, a flock
       of geese cleaned their summer-plumped bodies.

All that ocean and back to the same cutting waters.
               Green tufting out of the bonerock, air filled
       with the dead. Sunlight traces the fish-scaled roof

of the circus. *The family circus*, as we claimed. All that ocean
           and back to the same cutting waters. Family
      of metalsmiths who roofed this new city: I looked for our name.

Patricia Davis-Muffett
On Looking Away

If you sit on the couch, with your mother at your side,
her head in a silk scarf, hiding white stubble—
if she holds the Book of Common Prayer, the Bible,
the navy blue 1982 Hymnal containing her favorite songs,
you can always pretend she has not been planning
her funeral, is not trying to give you the chance
to say whatever is stuck in your throat, is not telling you
to brace yourself for what is coming—faster
than either of you imagined.

She lists the psalms, the order of lessons, hums her favorite hymns—
rehearsing, preparing. Two weeks and you will put her plans in place.

Instead, you can memorize the pattern
of the ivy-covered rug, the flowers intertwined,
you can search the glass-fronted cabinet
full of Hummel children—the ones she has labeled
under their feet, one for each grandchild, even the one
here in your belly, unusually quiet in his floating almost life today.

You can tell yourself that something will occur—
the *deus ex machina* you have begged for these long months,
the one you offered everything for—all of your chips to the middle:
"Here, take my future, my left hand, my unborn child."
None of it enough.

Instead of speaking, you can kneel at her feet,
offer to clip her toenails, the ones she can't reach,
the one thing she won't ask of her husband
who has looked in her eyes, held her hand
in the infusion room, in the hospital,
at the funeral parlor, with the hospice team.
You can do this one thing you hope says to her
what sticks in your throat is the howl
of love, the howl of despair.

Ava Winter

Lucky Jew

In Poland, folk carvings of Jews traditionally made by Christians are believed to bring good luck.

I am nothing but wood
you made to mean with a knife,
two springs for my feet,

a coat of paint. In my hands
you place a snippet of the Torah
you found hidden

in a crawlspace. Press
my black hat backward
and I rock, my prayer

frenetic as the guard dog
bounding on his own spring
by your daughter's doll house.

Every day you carve another Jew.
One of us holds a fiddle, another
holds a coin, but we all bear the face

of the baker's boy you half-
recall from childhood games,
though his nose has grown,

his back bent like your own
by years of carving. I wonder,
will you make enough of us

to form a minyan, enough to pray
the Kaddish, before you box us up,
before you ship us off to the shops?

Katherine Gaffney

Like a Salmon (Or Fool in a Blue House)

I feel like a fool in a blue house, thought I could curate
the life we'd live—repot herbs in spring, summer dinners
on the deck, year-round sex on the couch. Saturday
we'd bake bread. Sunday we'd walk in the sleepy
evening steadying ourselves for the week. But we've got
none of that, except for sex on the couch. He's bought
in, even with the front door open, weather permitting,
where extra quiet becomes a game we play. He says
his grandmother, in old age, was like a salmon,
wanting to return to Czechoslovakia, fuck, then die.
Fuck, then die, is a thought I've had in our bed—
how a woman in a too-large oxford shirt communicates
sex, for me, translates to never getting off
my my-size shirt. Please excuse the Post-it notes,
it's just the dishes are dry and could stand to be re-homed
or the mail has piled up again on the counter and I can't find
the surface. Perhaps it would be easier to write in a chorus.
I've gone about this all wrong—this is not chess or a set
of stringy marionettes where, if I leave the pieces for a day,
I can return to them unmoved.

Lupita Eyde-Tucker

Eucalyptus

In 1879 Presidente Garcia Moreno
brought silver dollar eucalyptus trees
from Australia

to dig their heels into these hills
to keep things from sliding   further.

*

In the foothills of the Andes,
in a hush of eucalyptus
gnarled and knuckled bark

beckons me—*lie down*
on pillows of *hojarasca*.

Forest floor soaks up noise,
sponge of days.

Streaks of sunlight anoint
this stained-glass cathedral.

Here you can inhale deeper
than you've ever breathed.

*

My *abuelita*, when her name was Deifilia
bundled eucalyptus branches on her way home,

hung their bouquets upside-down
until the cordillera rains would bring *el resfrío*.

In Guayaquil, when her name was Marianita,
when traditions were all she had left,

eucalyptus and manzanilla hung in her kitchen,
bought from *las indias en el Mercado Sur*.

Camouflaged in dark green leaves,
she shape-shifted into tropical hibiscus,

caged-bird-of-paradise pressed between
spiral bound pages. The crinkle of scripture,

fragrance of Vicks VapoRub, her sabbath rituals
the sacred aroma   that permeates everything.

*

The first time, I traveled there
in my father's Volkswagen camper

the patina on the leaves
reminded me of greenbacks,
copper pennies, the Statue of Liberty.

I wanted to be a forest ranger,
so I could spend all day

in that temple, branches lifted in praise—
lifted to hold back the sky.

*

I too have been uprooted
brought thousands of miles, expected
to thrive in foreign soil.

Decades later, I learn
eucalyptus trees suck all the water
from Andean aquifers.

My conscience pangs.
My roots are still thirsting.

*

Now, I still get congested, return
to lush Andean forests, my grandmother's home

release the trees into the air above my mug

Una aguita de eucalipto, mijita
Gracias, abuelita

I sip in the now, and breathe—
my ribcage the open and closed lung
of a blessed forest's unleaving.

Eric Yip

Fricatives

To speak English properly, Mrs. Lee said, you must learn
the difference between *three* and *free*. Three men
escaped from Alcatraz in a rubber raft and drowned
on their way to Angel Island. Hear the difference? Try
this: you fought your way into existence. Better. Look
at this picture. Fresh yellow grains beaten
till their seeds spill. That's threshing. That's
submission. You must learn to submit
before you can learn. You must be given
a voice before you can speak. Nobody wants to listen
to a spectacled boy with a Hong Kong accent.
You will have to leave this city, these dark furrows
stuffed full with ancestral bones. Know
that death is thorough. You will speak of bruised bodies
skinnier than yours, force the pen past batons
and blood, call it fresh material for writing. Now
they're paying attention. You're lucky enough
to care how the tongue moves, the seven types
of fricatives, the articulatory function of teeth
sans survival. You will receive a good education
abroad and make your parents proud. You will take
a stranger's cock in your mouth in the piss-slick stall
of that dingy Cantonese restaurant you love and taste
where you came from, what you were made of all along.
Put some work into it, he growls. *C'mon, give me
some bite.* Your mother visits one October, tells you
how everyone speaks differently here, more proper.

You smile, nod, bring her to your favorite restaurant,
order dim sum in English. They're releasing
the students arrested five years ago. *Just a tad more
soy sauce please, thank you.* The television replays
yesterday on repeat. The teapots are refilled. You spoon
served rice into your mouth, this perfect rice.
Steamed, perfect, white.

Caleb Braun

Self-Portrait as Yard Boy

What I learned of loneliness I learned mostly
mowing the lawn. August; Texas dusk; finally
not too hot to push a rotting motor through

the dry grass of a quarter-acre backyard. Tall fence,
a few trees, shapes of neighbors shadowing the gaps.
We'd speak to each other when the fence was broken.

Otherwise, there I was alone knowing my dad
wanted the grass an inch shorter but the clouds,
at least, were heavenly, heaven-sent—they filled, I mean, the bland

oppressive sky with pink, like cotton candy
at a funeral. And why did I feel guilty then
as I do now watching the season

start saying again *spring* with specks of wildflowers—
plains paintbrush, Blackfoot daisy. It should be as easy:
grown, the mind tilled of its infertile habits.

The wish to go, for example, to my Father and confess
I only wanted to hear *well done*
my good and faithful servant or at least my name

called as a dog's would have been
if we owned one. Well, there was for a moment Buddy,
Collie the color of a cow, rioting like mad

in our too close yard. And maybe they weren't lying,
maybe they took him out to the farm: generic, boundless,
as true as a math equation. Maybe they'd only left out

how he loved us, how he turned upon encountering
fields forever back toward the blue Windstar
with the sliding door he emerged from wanting

to go back home. So, this is not a prayer but an elegy.
The "I" one sets off like a plot of land
grows smaller each year. The names

I'd thought would scatter like clippings
from an unfinished childhood have rooted
and bloomed: Buddy: rowdy-in-the-tall-grass;

Moses, goofy-eyed and shy, juking in the volleyball sand;
and Goldie, here, in the pollinated afternoon air,
shaggy-haired-terrier rolling her barrel body

in the lawn—let this be one
of the many of her memories that seed
in my synapses. Only the necessary

remains. I, for example, still must say I,
though I'm not that boy anymore
and now suspect I never was.

Anny Tang
My Mother

a child again. I trace blue-soft tremors
       of her eyelids like veins of silk leaves,
her longing for a riptide of sleep
       that doesn't arrive. how she once
waited at my bedside in lush darkness,
       her arm pulled to my belly like an oar.
the way villagers lay sacks of rice
       on restless toddlers, the weight
dragging them to the still depths
       of a dream. whether her myth or memory,
I never learned. now I touch her mottled
       temple, a burial of singed nerves. her mouth
dried persimmon, language carved
       clean like a pit. at dawn, I feed her congee
from soft spoons & her hands collapse
       to her heart, an inelegant gratitude.
Oh Mom—there are people not meant for
       this life & I am one. my future nothing
but your old promise: our faces withering
       twin-like & together in coffee shops, rinsed
in tinsel glow of fleeting Novembers. but now
       you're gone already. here, but lost
behind ashen eyes. will you ever
       smile at me again like before—
that summer in Hainan, our ankles marbled
       in the sea. how you laughed, pulling me close
under a shawl of milk-stained night

Abriana Jetté
Thinking of Instinct

Some geese just won't leave.
Beaks dipped beneath snow and sleet
even when their beloved lake freezes
they don't leave. They find some unfrozen piece
of water and land, picking at winter wheat
or whatever is left for them to eat.
They learn to survive, he says, thinking it sweet
how they stick around. Not me.

It's not sweet, I say, but instinct. Or lack thereof.
No flight or fight when you can't perceive leaving.
Sure, they survive, but is that really enough?
We walk in circles around the park. It's sweet
until it isn't. Some things are worth quitting.
These geese don't know what they're missing.

Colin Bailes
Bluegrass

Even though there was a calmness to their grazing—

a tenderness, even—I couldn't help but think of the centaurs

unused to wine, their wild nature

come to fore, how they attempted to kidnap Hippodameia, *tamer*

of horses, and the ensuing battle—

how the Lapiths, inventors of the bridle, defeated

their rageful, drunken guests.

These horses, blurring the line, once again, between desire

and need, slaking hunger

on bluegrass; *this not being able to assign what's missing*

some shape, a name; and me, standing in a field, waiting

on a brown bird to break from bristlegrass and, like dandelion seed

blown loose by breeze, dissolve near the horizon.

Do you think they woke ashamed—

the centaurs, I mean—riddled with remorse for all they had done?

Kieron Walquist

You, Me, Frank Hayes, Sweet Kiss

My favorite record: in 1923, a dead man won a steeplechase. Which was also his first race.

> I come out to my parents + you dump me in a text.

The stable hand turned stand-in jockey was Frank Hayes. The horse, a seven-year-old mare,
    was named Sweet Kiss. It was also her first race.

Your text: *I'm sorry you're feeling this kind of loneliness. I also want to let you know that lately I've been feeling
    a little emotionally unavailable/detached from the world—*

During the race, Hayes [either 22 or 35, according to some newspapers] suffered a heartattack.

Your text: *You've been so good to me, + I've done my best to recipoocate—but despite that, I don't feel
    the romantic "spark."*

He slumped over, but remained in the saddle. Sweet Kiss kept running + crossed the finish line.

> The odds: 20–1.

> I thought our odds were greater.

Your text: *I know we talked some before I left, but did we really talk about what we wanted from each other?*

At the finish line, it's said a small crowd ran out to congratuale the two.

> Hayes, then, against the horse's neck, fell.

Before you left, I stayed with you + helped you pack. Helped you throw this + that out
      in the alleyway dumpster.

While some say Frank's heart failed from excitement, others believe it was a result of having
      to lose ten pounds in twenty-four hours, reducing his weight to 130 pounds.

I bought groceries that week. What you didn't pitch, you put back in my hands.

I ate grapes, pickles. Poptarts, granola bars, potato chips, + those yogurt popsicles you asked for
      on my car ride home.

                        I no longer had a home, then.

Your text: *I didn't really know how I felt [regarding the spark being gone for me] until you were helping me*
      move, + then I didn't know how to communicate that to you.

Out of respect for Hayes, Belmont's jockey club still declared him the winner.

Three days later, he was buried in the same riding silks.

Sometimes, I wear the briefs you mailed me. They're yellow + too small.

                     We haven't spoken since September.

During the race, as Hayes cleared the final jump + passed the winning posts, spectators
      took his leaning for love, believed he'd been whispering in the mare's ear.

My second favorite record: being buried alive was so common in the nineteenth century, doctors
      would tie a string to a person's finger, + if that person were to wake up + move,
      the string would ring a bell outside the coffin.

                  Before you left, you kissed me goodbye outside a coffee shop.

Sweet Kiss, after June fourth, never found another rider due to superstition. Retired after one race.

        Tell me, bub: which one of us is the horse + which one the jockey?

For us, should the jockey be called *honesty*?

Is the horse named *heartache*?

        The other night, I heard a bell in the dark.

        Wanted it to be you. Wanted it to be my mother.

After June fourth, Sweet Kiss was known as *Sweet Kiss of Death*.

Tell me, bub: is our horse fed peppermint + led out to pasture?

        Is our horse on a carousel, meant to run a race that never ceases?

        Only circles.

Jalen Eutsey
West Perrine Park (The Big Park)

> *It gave these Black men their poetry.*
> —Howard Bryant

A white boy asked me to walk him to the bathroom before
a baseball game at a public park where my father was once

pseudonymed myth, he (Eight The Snake), and a generation
of Hellcats (Peewee, Crow, Rome, Termite, and others), had

been good for pockets and bad for business as fans won
ends on the weekend, betting and rooting for the home team—

everyone in their Easter Sunday, straight-from-the-pew,
alabaster best (or home whites), swaying behind home plate

and sprinkled down the right field line like sea foam teasing
the shore—then decided to opt out of the grinding march

of money-making come Monday; what the boy seemed too
afraid to understand, was that all the men crowding around

the teal, worn-metal bleachers behind the dugout, were arguing
about the Dolphins or playing the dozens or sipping grape soda

or rolling bones or narrating the sweat-ballet unfurling atop
the two-toned green and pink-red basketball court and all

those men would soon be rooting for him because he was
wearing orange and green; what was unseen were the tightened

black backs of the men that built the field he could now
extend his dreams on; I think he homered that day, rounding

the bases with a surprised smile as the Hellcats of old tapered
a fade or faded from memory; he always played better on this

hallowed ground he couldn't divorce from phantom echoes
of bullets and blood. I walked the boy across the second, unused

court to the bathroom, our metal cleats tapping a tune of pregame
buzz and jitters, while a mother weaved box braids into her daughter's

hair down the left field line and the memories of a *Milk Man*
with no milk, hung like fog in the air around the backstop—

Bubble Gum Stadium they called it.

Suzanne Langlois

Denouement

The only part of *Time Bandits* I remember
is the end, when the boy's parents hold
a toaster oven between them with a charred
hunk of evil inside. The boy tells them
not to touch it. I think he says, "Don't touch it,
it's evil!" But they touch it anyway, and though
we don't like them—they're bad parents—
the resulting blast is disturbing. Even as
the curious neighbors step out onto their lawns
and the firetrucks arrive, we know he'll be left
alone, which isn't necessarily better. I might
be remembering it wrong. It's been thirty years
since I saw it. But I remember clearly the dull
sense of dread settling in my bones. It probably
came from the recent realization that my parents
weren't quite up to the task of raising me,
and that I wasn't quite up to it either,
and those were the only available options.
This was about the time when all my friends'
parents decided it would be best if I played
at their houses, and not the other way around.
They were generous with their invitations
to sleepovers, but it was starting to dawn
on me that that's what this was—generosity—
and generosity was something people exercised
when they were comfortable and had some
comfort to spare. It other words, it was optional,

conditional, and unreliable. Our toaster oven
was reliable. I used it to cook Pop-Tarts and
English muffin pizzas, which, along with ramen,
were the main staples of my diet. I was trying
to grow up as quickly as I could. I didn't know
how much time I had left before it all exploded,
leaving me like the boy in the movie, standing
alone in the front yard as the sirens faded
and everyone else went back inside.

Kenzie Allen
Quiet as Thunderbolts

And I kept it from you like a kill,
my name, my legacy, my shoulder
chip and the small hollow beneath

where I can be wounded. The Longhouse
I whittled to matchsticks, abalone
filling up with hair ties, Ute painted

coffee mugs and iron turtles a pan-flash
of identity, an almond eye watching
from between the white bookcases

and photographs of cities, orchards,
graves. A lonely ironing board
left to the street outside our old place,

candles I lit in church for all the women
I have loved. Animals who are no longer
with us. Animals who are no longer

ours. So much landscape I can't
tend to, wide as a child's face
and crumbled in drought,

rimmed in salt. I kept the Water
Lily, how Bear Clan was given
the medicines, Namegiver,

how she made me darker
with her words. The turquoise ring
and how it pleases the Spirits

to give that which has been
so admired. The sweetgrass
in my sock drawer, the exact volume

of air I can fit in my lungs and belly
as I try to swallow and breathe
its sweetness. Every bead, every

loop of every treasure necklace—
I kept porcupine quills
in my throat, I let the water drown me

every night in my river-bottom
canoe. I've been sleepwalking
since I got to this earth,

since they brought up the soil
and made an island, those who did not perish
in the dive. Since the island crawled

into a continent, I've been
shell and memory, calendar and hearth.

T. R. Poulson

Birds Never Nest Here

> *after Richard Hugo's* The Triggering Town

You've never heard of my town. It straddles
Forgotten River, where the Main Street Trestle,
now broken, once crossed. Now a ferry paddles
back and forth, Sundays. On the west
side stands the butcher's shop, the tenderest meats,
on the east, his wife picks grapes and cherries,
bakes pies to feed her other lover, a concrete
mixer. We pray at dinner here. Barges carry
guests of every faith to our downtown docks.
We put down pillows and towels in spare
guest rooms, serve pancakes, and ancient books.
We pray. Those who don't repent just disappear.
It's a mystery where the butcher finds his prey,
the nearest ranch, four hundred miles away.

Esther Lin
Habit

My husband's favorite is to suffer.
I too have taken this up;

I pant for what I can't have.
The world is full of trite regard.

Those who love lightly as houseflies
do so because they expect calamity,

and those who love passionately
demand a righting of ancient wrongs.

My mother did both.
Her voice high and keen

from the bed she routinely took ill.
I brought her pills; she shared them

with me and I went off into my own life,
fearing and trusting everyone.

M.A. Nicholson

Dandies, Wilde

after Robin Coste Lewis's "The Wilde Woman of Aiken"

You cannot prevent us / from casting sun / flowers to seed
at the fence (hedging / a border trap / crop for diamond

backed stink / bugs) mustard / greens thick
unruly at our feet / harboring snail / orgies orange leaf

footed nymphs / are welcomed / we cast
your brocades aside / slip shoes off / at the door

dig the clay / deep / where the water
table rises / spin earth / en vessels

our voices are / sitting in / the open
glow of swelling / night / shades in rows

keep your corn / keep your measures / this spring
you'll find / only / broken

vases and gates / flung rusted / against your march
may we weave / the dried invasives / under no one's

watchful eye / fill them / with eager
with spicy radish / harbored by / pickling

cucumber vine / okra welcoming / the sugar
ants to our west / a million / underfoot

we don't bury our dead / we house them / behind welded
iron curling / still listening / dark

welcomes / what has always / existed
you try / try try / but you

can never / stamp / our abundance

          —Nominated by University of New Orleans Creative Writing Workshop

Katie Farris
Why Write Love Poetry in a Burning World

To train myself to find, in the midst of hell
what isn't hell

The body, bald, cancerous, but still
beautiful enough to
imagine living the body
washing the body
replacing a loose front
porch step the body chewing
what it takes to keep a body
going—

this scene has a tune
a language I can read
this scene has a door
I cannot close I stand
within its wedge
I stand within its shield

Why write love poetry in a burning world?
To train myself, in the midst of a burning world,
to offer poems of love to a burning world.

Jennifer Loyd

I Want to Tell Rachel Carson about Centralia, Pennsylvania, and Twenty-Four-Hour Gas Stations

Take desire, for example.
She was always searching for
the hidden entrance
in the trunk of the riven tree.
One minute mistletoe is a parasite,
the next, a collaborator.
I imagine the entanglement of all
energy on its way to outer space
must sound, to the Universe,
like the music playing in line
for Space Mountain.
Imagine all the things I've thrown away
in gas station bathrooms—
like the thrice-wrapped pregnancy test
taken at four a.m.—
imagine how they must share space in the atmosphere
with the ash of the letters she burned.

—Nominated by *Poet Lore*

Acknowledgments

Sarah Ghazal Ali's "Parable of Flies" previously appeared in *The Adroit Journal*.

Kenzie Allen's "Quiet as Thunderbolts" previously appeared in *The Paris Review*'s *The Daily*.

Amy M. Alvarez's "Hadeology" previously appeared in *Ploughshares*.

Arao Ameny's "The Mothers" previously appeared in *World Literature Today*.

Colin Bailes's "Bluegrass" previously appeared in *Subtropics*.

Caleb Braun's "Self-Portrait as Yard Boy" previously appeared in *Blackbird*.

Kōan Brink's "Self-Portrait as Lake" previously appeared in *Washington Square Review*.

Madeleine Cravens's "Creation Myth" previously appeared in *Raleigh Review*.

Patricia Davis-Muffett's "On Looking Away" previously appeared in *Comstock Review*.

Steven Espada Dawson's "Elegy for the Four Chambers of My Brother's Heart" previously appeared in *Poetry*.

Fay Dillof's "Little Infinites" previously appeared in *The Gettysburg Review*.

Kinsale Drake's "Blacklist Me" previously appeared in *poets.org*.

Sara Elkamel's "In This Town We Rescue Cats" previously appeared in *Salamander Magazine*.

Jalen Eutsey's "West Perrine Park (The Big Park)" previously appeared in *The Adroit Journal*.

Lupita Eyde-Tucker's "Eucalyptus" previously appeared in *Philadelphia Stories*.

Katie Farris's "Why Write Love Poetry in a Burning World" previously appeared in *A Net to Catch My Body in Its Weaving*, a chapbook by *Beloit Poetry Journal*.

J. Bruce Fuller's "They Said" previously appeared in *The Southern Review*.

Katherine Gaffney's "Like a Salmon (Or Fool in a Blue House)" previously appeared in the magazine *Lost Pilots* and *Once Read as Ruin*, a chapbook by Finishing Line Press.

Maria Gray's "Where Were You When Mac Miller Died" previously appeared in *Snaggletooth Magazine*.

Justin Groppuso-Cook's "How I Learned to Drink Oni, the Bitter Vine of Knowledge" previously appeared in *Crab Creek Review*.

Abriana Jetté's "Thinking of Instinct" previously appeared in *Third Wednesday Magazine*.

Ashley Keyser's "Eating the Siren" previously appeared in *Copper Nickel*.

Willie Lee Kinard III's "A Tangle of Gorgons" previously appeared in *Poetry* and *The Columbia Granger's World of Poetry*.

Peter LaBerge's "Sight of Love" previously appeared in *Crazyhorse*.

Suzanne Langlois's "Denouement" previously appeared in *Rust + Moth*.

Esther Lin's "Habit" previously appeared in *The Cortland Review*.

Jennifer Loyd's "I Want to Tell Rachel Carson about Centralia, Pennsylvania, and Twenty-Four-Hour Gas Stations" previously appeared in *Poet Lore*.

Grace MacNair's "Necessity Is the Mother of Invention" previously appeared in *Inch #52*, a micro-chapbook by Bull City Press.

james mckenna's "Long" previously appeared in *poets.org*.

Madeleine Mori's "Tachistoscope" previously appeared in *The Yale Review*.

Alixen Pham's "The Burden of Translation" previously appeared in *Salamander*.

T. R. Poulson's "Birds Never Nest Here" previously appeared in *Poets Speaking to Poets: Echoes and Tributes*.

Jacob Anthony Ramírez's "The Lives of Jazz Fathers" previously appeared in *Kitchen Boombox*, a chapbook by Ignition Press.

Cyndie Randall's "J" previously appeared in *the minnesota review*

Anny Tang's "My Mother" previously appeared in *Grain*.

Brandon Thurman's "New Moon Ceremony" previously appeared in *Frontier Poetry*.

Ross White's "Mule" previously appeared in *Ploughshares*.

Ava Winter's "Lucky Jew" previously appeared in *TriQuarterly*.

Eric Yip's "Fricatives" previously appeared in *The Poetry Review*.

Mariya Zilberman's "Yanka Kupala Street" previously appeared in *Kenyon Review Online*.

Contributors' Notes

SARAH GHAZAL ALI is the author of *Theophanies* (Alice James Books, 2024), selected as the Editors' Choice for the 2022 Alice James Award. A Djanikian Scholar, her poems appear in *Poetry*, *American Poetry Review*, *Pleiades*, *The Rumpus*, *Electric Literature*, and elsewhere. She has received support from Community of Writers, the Kenyon Review Writers Workshop, Hambidge Center, and the University of Massachusetts Amherst. She lives in Lewisburg, Pennsylvania, where she is a Stadler Fellow at Bucknell University and poetry editor for *West Branch*. Learn more at sarahgali.com.

KENZIE ALLEN is a Haundenosaunee poet and multimodal artist, and a descendant of the Oneida Nation of Wisconsin. She is the recipient of a 92NY Discovery Prize, the 49th Parallel Award in Poetry, and a James Welch Prize for Indigenous Poets. A finalist for the National Poetry Series, she is a graduate of the creative writing PhD at University of Wisconsin–Milwaukee and the Helen Zell Writers Program MFA at the University of Michigan. Her work can be found in *Narrative*, *Poetry*, *Boston Review*, *poets.org*, and other venues.

AMY M. ALVAREZ is a Black Latinx poet and educator. Her poems have appeared in *Ploughshares*, *The Missouri Review*, *Crazyhorse*, *Colorado Review*, and elsewhere. Amy is a CantoMundo, VONA, and Macondo Fellow. In 2022, she was inducted as an Affrilachian Poet. Amy lives and teaches in West Virginia. For more, please visit amymalavarez.com.

ARAO AMENY is a U.S.-based writer and poet from Lango, Northern Uganda. Her first published poem, "Home is a Woman," won *The Southern Review*'s 2020 James Olney Award. She was a winner of the 2021 Brooklyn Poets Fellowship, a finalist for the UK-based 2021 Brunel International African Poetry Prize, and a 2021 *Best New Poets* nominee. She is an alumna of the Kenyon Review Writers Workshop (poetry) and Tin House Workshop (fiction writing). Her poetry appears in *The Southern Review* and *World Literature Review*. Her short story is forthcoming in *Relations: An Anthology of African and Diaspora Voices*. She earned an MFA in fiction writing from the University of Baltimore, an MA in journalism from Indiana University, and a BA in political science from the University of Indianapolis. For more, please visit araoameny.com.

CLARESSINKA ANDERSON's poems and essays have appeared in or are forthcoming from *The Los Angeles Review of Books, Autre Magazine, bedfellows, Chiron Review, Contemporary Art Review Los Angeles* (*Carla*), and elsewhere, as well as in the anthology, *Choice Words: Writers on Abortion* (Haymarket Books, 2020). Through her ongoing collaborations with artists, her work engages the interstitial spaces of contemporary art, literature, and music. Anderson holds an MFA in poetry from Bennington College. Born and raised in London, she lives in Los Angeles and dreams about rain.

COLIN BAILES is originally from Orlando, Florida. A 2022 National Poetry Series finalist, his work has appeared or is forthcoming in *Blackbird, The Cortland Review, Missouri Review, Narrative, Raleigh Review, Subtropics,* and *wildness,* among other journals. He holds an MFA from Virginia Commonwealth University, where he served as the 2020–2021 Levis Reading Prize Fellow and was awarded the Catherine and Joan Byrne Poetry Prize from the Academy of American Poets. He lives and teaches in Gainesville, Florida. For more, please visit colinbailes.com.

CALEB BRAUN earned an MFA in poetry from the University of Washington, where he received the Harold Taylor Prize. He is a PhD student in creative writing at Texas Tech University in Lubbock, Texas. His poems have appeared and are forthcoming in *The Gettysburg Review, 32 Poems, Image, Blackbird, Verse Daily,* and elsewhere. He can be found online at calebbraun.com.

KŌAN BRINK was born and raised in Minnesota. They are a lay-ordained Zen student and teacher. They are the author of a chapbook of poems, *The End of Lake Superior* (above/ground, 2021) and an artist's book, *What Sleeps under Lacquer* (NECK Press, 2022). They received their MFA from Columbia University, where they were also a Teaching Fellow and studied Buddhist texts and social ethics at Union Theological Seminary. They currently live in Austin, Texas, with their partner and rescue husky.

MADELEINE CRAVENS is a Wallace Stegner Fellow at Stanford University. She received her MFA from Columbia University, where she was a recipient of the Max Ritvo Fellowship. She was the first place winner of *Narrative*'s thirteenth annual poetry contest and 2020 30 Below contest. She is from Brooklyn and currently lives in Oakland.

PATRICIA DAVIS-MUFFETT (she/her) holds an MFA from the University of Minnesota. Her chapbook, *alchemy of yeast and tears,* is forthcoming. Her work has won numerous honors including a *Best of the Net* 2022 nomination and second place in the 2022 Joe Gouveia Outermost Poetry Contest and has appeared in *Atlanta Review*, *Pretty Owl Poetry*, *Calyx* and *Comstock Review*, among others. She lives in Rockville, Maryland, with her family.

STEVEN ESPADA DAWSON is from East Los Angeles and lives in Madison, Wisconsin, where he is the Jay C. and Ruth Halls Fellow in Poetry at the Wisconsin Institute for Creative Writing. The son of a Mexican immigrant, he is the recipient of a Pushcart Prize and a Ruth Lilly and Dorothy Sargent Rosenberg Poetry Fellowship. Most recently, his work appears in *AGNI*, *Guernica*, *Kenyon Review*, *Ninth Letter*, and *Poetry*.

FAY DILLOF's poetry has appeared in *Gettysburg Review*, *Ploughshares*, *Spillway*, *FIELD*, *Rattle*, *New Ohio Review*, and elsewhere. Her writing has been supported by scholarships from Bread Loaf, Sewanee, and Napa Valley Writers' Conference. She's been awarded the Milton Kessler Memorial Prize for Poetry and the Dogwood Literary Prize in Poetry. Fay lives with her husband and daughter in Northern California where she works as a psychotherapist.

KINSALE DRAKE is a Diné poet and playwright based in the Southwest. Her work has appeared in *poets.org*, *The Adroit Journal*, *Time*, NPR, MTV, and elsewhere. She recently graduated from Yale University with a BA in English and Ethnicity, Race, and Migration, where she won a Yale Indigenous Performing Arts Program prize, the Young Native Playwrights Award, the J. Edgar Meeker Prize, and an Academy of American Poets Prize. Currently, she is an inaugural Indigenous Nations Poets Fellow. You can visit her at kinsaledrake.com.

SARA ELKAMEL is a poet and journalist living between her hometown, Cairo, and New York City. She holds an MA in arts journalism from Columbia University, and an MFA in poetry from New York University. Elkamel's poems have appeared in *Poetry Magazine*, *The Common*, *Michigan Quarterly Review*, *Four Way Review*, *The Yale Review*, *The Cincinnati Review*, *Gulf Coast*, *Poetry London*, *Poet Lore*, and elsewhere. Her work has also been featured as part of the anthologies *Best of the Net 2020*, *The BreakBeat Poets Vol. 3: Halal If You Hear Me*, and *20.35 Africa: Vol. 2*. She was named a 2020 Gregory Djanikian Scholar by *The Adroit Journal*, and a finalist in *Narrative*'s 30 Below Contest in the same year. Elkamel's debut chapbook *Field of No Justice* was published by the African Poetry Book Fund and Akashic Books in 2021.

JALEN EUTSEY is a 2022–2024 Wallace Stegner fellow at Stanford University. His poems have appeared in *The Hopkins Review*, *Poetry Northwest*, *Nashville Review*, *Harpur Palate*, and elsewhere. He received an MFA from The Writing Seminars at Johns Hopkins University, where he also taught creative writing to young adults through the Writers in Baltimore Schools and Baltimore Youth Film Arts programs. He was born and raised in Miami, Florida.

LUPITA EYDE-TUCKER was born in New Jersey and raised in Guayaquil, Ecuador, where she began writing and translating poetry in English and Spanish. Her poems have appeared in *Nashville Review*, *Columbia Journal*, *Raleigh Review*, *Women's Voices for Change*, *[PANK]*, *American Life in Poetry*, *The Cortland Review*, and *Ninth Letter*. Since 2018 she has been translating Venezuelan poet Oriette D'Angelo. Lupita is pursuing an MFA in poetry at the University of Florida, and has received fellowships and institutional support from Kentucky Women Writers Conference, Bread Loaf Writers Conferences, the New York State Summer Writers Institute, and Vermont Studio Center. Read more here: NotEnoughPoetry.com

KATIE FARRIS is the author of *A Net to Catch My Body in Its Weaving*, winner of the 2021 Chad Walsh Poetry Award, and her collection of poems, *Standing in the Forest of Being Alive*, is forthcoming from Alice James Books in 2023. She is also the author of the hybrid-form text *boysgirls* (Marick Press, 2011 and Tupelo Press, 2019) and the chapbooks *Thirteen Intimacies* (Fivehundred Places, 2017) and *Mother Superior in Hell* (Dancing Girl, 2019). Most recently she is winner of poetry awards from *Beloit Poetry Journal*, *Fairy Tale Review*, *Massachusetts Review*, and the Orison Anthology Prize in Fiction. Her work has appeared *American Poetry Review*, *Granta*, *The Atlantic Monthly*, *The Nation*, and *Poetry*, and has been commissioned by MoMA. She is the co-translator of several books of poetry from the French, Chinese, and Russian, including *Gossip and Metaphysics: Russian Modernist Poems and Prose*. She graduated with an MFA from Brown University, and is currently an associate professor of literature, media, and communication at Georgia Institute of Technology.

J. BRUCE FULLER is the author of *How to Drown a Boy* (forthcoming, 2024 LSU Press). His chapbooks include *The Dissenter's Ground*, *Lancelot*, and *Flood*, and his poems have appeared at *The Southern Review*, *Crab Orchard Review*, *McNeese Review*, *Birmingham Poetry Review*, and *Louisiana Literature*, among others. He has received scholarships from Bread Loaf, the Sewanee Writers' Conference, and Stanford University, where he was a Wallace Stegner Fellow. He teaches at Sam Houston State University where he is director of Texas Review Press.

KATHERINE GAFFNEY completed her MFA at the University of Illinois at Urbana–Champaign and is currently working on her PhD at the University of Southern Mississippi. Her work has previously appeared in *jubilat*, *Harpur Palate*, *Mississippi Review*, *Meridian*, and elsewhere. She has attended the Tin House

Summer Writing Workshop, the SAFTA Residency, and the Sewanee Writers Conference as a scholar. Her first chapbook, *Once Read as Ruin*, was published by Finishing Line Press. Her first full-length poetry collection is forthcoming from Tampa University Press in 2023 after winning the Tampa Review Prize for Poetry.

BENJAMIN GOLDBERG's poems have appeared or are forthcoming in *Poetry TriQuarterly*, *West Branch*, *Blackbird*, *Best New Poets 2014* and *2020*, *Verse Daily*, and elsewhere. He lives with his wife outside Washington, D.C.

MARIA GRAY is a poet, student, and 2000s baby from Portland, Oregon. Her work appears in *SICK*, *The Lumiere Review*, *Kissing Dynamite Poetry*, and others, and she has received honors from organizations including *The Lumiere Review*, *The Adroit Journal*, Oregon Poetry Association, Bates College, and the National Federation of State Poetry Societies. She reads for *Counterclock Journal* and lives in Lewiston, Maine, where she studies English at Bates College. Find her at mariagray.carrd.co.

JUSTIN GROPPUSO-COOK is a writer-in-residence at InsideOut Literary Arts Project and poetry reader for *West Trade Review*. His poems have appeared or are forthcoming in *Bear Review*, *Luna Luna Magazine*, *Crab Creek Review*, and *EcoTheo Review*, among others. He received the 2021 Haunted Waters Press Award for Poetry. His chapbook, *Our Illuminated Pupils*, was a semi-finalist for the Tomaž Šalamun Prize (Factory Hollow Press). In 2022, he was a resident at Writing Workshops Paris. More information can be found on his website, sunnimani.com.

KALEEM HAWA writes about art, film, and literature. His poems have been previously published in *The Poetry Review*, *The New Republic*, and *The White Review*.

Born and raised in Brooklyn, New York, ABRIANA JETTÉ is an internationally published poet and essayist whose work has appeared in *Plume*, *The Moth*, *River Teeth*, *Poetry New Zealand*, and many other places. Abriana has received fellowships from the Southampton Writers Conference, the Community of Writers at Squaw Valley, and the Sewanee Writers Conference. She teaches at Kean University.

KUHU JOSHI is originally from New Delhi, India. Her work appears in *Rattle*, *petrichor*, *The Yearbook of Indian Poetry*, *The Bombay Literary Magazine*, and elsewhere. She received her MFA from Sarah Lawrence College, where she was a recipient of the Jane Cooper Poetry Fellowship and was awarded an honorable mention for the John B. Santoianni Award by the Academy of American Poets. She currently teaches in New York.

ASHLEY KEYSER lives in Chicago, where she is currently working on a collection about colors and queer desire. Her poetry has appeared in *The Adroit Journal, Pleiades, Quarterly West, Copper Nickel*, and elsewhere.

WILLIE LEE KINARD III (he/they) is a poet, designer, educator, and musician forged in Newberry, South Carolina, and the author of *Orders of Service* (Alice James Books, 2023), winner of the 2022 Alice James Award. With written work appearing or forthcoming in *Obsidian, Boston Review, Poetry, The Rumpus,* and elsewhere, he received his MFA in creative writing from the University of Pittsburgh and has received fellowships and support from The Watering Hole and The Pittsburgh Foundation. Go see 'bout them at williekinard.com.

PETER LaBERGE is the author of the chapbooks *Makeshift Cathedral* (YesYes Books) and *Hook* (Sibling Rivalry Press). His poetry has received a Pushcart Prize and has appeared in *AGNI, American Poetry Review, Kenyon Review, New England Review, Pleiades*, and *ZYZZYVA*, among others. Peter is the founder and editor-in-chief of *The Adroit Journal*, as well as an MFA candidate and Writers in the Public Schools Fellow at New York University.

SUZANNE LANGLOIS's collection *Bright Glint Gone* won the 2019 Maine Writers and Publishers Alliance chapbook award. Her poems have recently appeared in *Quarterly West, Rust + Moth, Whale Road Review, Scoundrel Time*, and *Leon Literary Review*. She holds a MFA from Warren Wilson College. Originally from Vermont, she now lives and teaches high school English in Maine.

KENT LEATHAM (he/him) is a poet, translator, and educator. His work has appeared in dozens of journals and anthologies in the United States and abroad, including *Ploughshares, Prairie Schooner, Poetry Quarterly*, and *Fence*. He studied poetry at Emerson College and Pacific Lutheran University, taught writing at California State University Monterey Bay for nine years, and currently facilitates the Monterey Bay Poetry Consortium reading series. He is proudly pansexual.

ESTHER LIN was born in Rio de Janeiro, Brazil, and lived in the United States as an undocumented immigrant for twenty-one years. She is the author of *The Ghost Wife*, winner of the 2017 Poetry Society of America Chapbook Fellowship. In 2020 she was a Writing Fellow at the Fine Arts Work Center, Provincetown, and from 2017 to 2019, a Wallace Stegner Fellow at Stanford University. She has received honors from the T. S. Eliot House; Cité internationale, Paris; the *Crab Orchard Review*; and Poets House. Currently she co-organizes the Undocupoets, which raises consciousness about the structural barriers undocumented poets face in the literary community.

Jennifer Loyd is a poet, translator, and a former editor for *Copper Nickel*, *West Branch*, and *Sycamore Review*. For her poetry exploring the archives of Rachel Carson, she has received a Stadler Fellowship, as well as travel grants for research from Purdue University, where she earned an MFA. Her poems and prose, which explore the intersection between private voice and public narratives, appear in *The Southern Review*, *The Rumpus*, *Shenandoah*, *Prairie Schooner*, *Poet Lore*, and elsewhere.

Grace MacNair is a poet, teacher, and healthcare professional living in Brooklyn, New York. She holds a BA from UNC Chapel Hill and an MFA from Hunter College. Grace was selected by Yona Harvey as the winner of *Radar Poetry*'s 2021 Coniston Prize and by Safia Elhillo as the winner of *Palette Poetry*'s 2022 Emerging Poet Prize. Her poems have appeared or are forthcoming in *The Threepenny Review*, *Radar Poetry*, *Palette Poetry*, *The Missouri Review*, and elsewhere. Grace's micro-chapbook, *Even As They Curse U*s, is available from Bull City Press. You can visit her at gracemacnair.com.

James mckenna is a writer in Alabama. They are editor of *Black Warrior Review* and their poems appear in *The Adroit Journal*, *poets.org*, *Quarterly West*, and elsewhere. They manage a small grocery store in town.

Madeleine Mori is a Japanese American writer and editor, born and raised in the San Francisco Bay Area. She earned a BS in wine and viticulture from California Polytechnic University San Luis Obispo and an MFA from New York University. Her work has appeared or is forthcoming in *jubilat*, *DIAGRAM*, *The American Poetry Review*, *The Yale Review*, *The Common*, *The Margins*, and elsewhere. She was a 2021 Margins Fellow through the Asian American Writers' Workshop, where she guest-edited a special folio on wine, and was the founding poetry editor at *Pigeon Pages*. She lives in Brooklyn and is the assistant director of the MFA in Writing at Sarah Lawrence College.

M.A. Nicholson is a New Orleans poet, editor, and educator. Her writing appears or is forthcoming in *Tilted House Review*, *Diode Poetry Journal*, *New Orleans Review*, *Talking River Review*, and elsewhere. An alumna of Loyola University and a MFA graduate from the University of New Orleans—where she served as associate poetry editor for *Bayou Magazine*—M.A. was the recipient of the 2021 Andrea-Saunders Gereighty

Academy of American Poets Award and is the co-founder of lmnl lit, an arts organization focused on offering free workshops, readings, and residencies. Connect with her at michellenicholsonpoetry.com

ALIXEN PHAM is a *Best of the Net*–nominated poet/writer/artist with various publications including *The Slowdown* featuring Ada Limon, *Salamander, Rust + Moth, Apogee Journal, New York Quarterly, Brooklyn Poets, DiaCRITICS, the museum of americana,* and *Gyroscope.* She leads the Westside Los Angeles chapter of Women Who Submit, a nonprofit organization nurturing and supporting women and non-binary writers. Alixen is the recipient of The City of West Hollywood Artist Grant, Brooklyn Poets Fellowship & Scholarship, AWP Mentee Program, PEN Center Fiction Scholarship and others. Her Twitter / Instagram is @AlixenPham.

T. R. POULSON, a University of Nevada alum and proud Wolf Pack fan, lives in San Mateo, California. Her poems and stories have appeared in various journals, including *Booth, Solstice, Aethlon, Jabberwock Review, Rattle,* and *New Verse News.* She is currently seeking a publisher for her first poetry collection, tentatively titled *Branded.*

GAIA RAJAN is the author of the chapbooks *Moth Funerals* (Glass Poetry Press 2020) and *Killing It* (Black Lawrence Press 2022). Her work is published in the 2022 *Best of the Net* anthology, *Kenyon Review, THRUSH, Split Lip Magazine,* and elsewhere. Gaia is an undergraduate at Carnegie Mellon University, studying computer science and creative writing. You can find her at @gaiarajan on Twitter or Instagram, or at gaiarajan.com.

JACOB ANTHONY RAMÍREZ is a poet and educator. He is a distinguished graduate from the University of Lancaster's Creative Writing MA where his is currently a PhD candidate. His debut pamphlet, *Kitchen Boombox,* was released by Oxford Brookes University's ignitionpress in 2022. Ramírez's poetry appears in several publications among them Haymarket Book's *The Breakbeat Poets Vol. IV, LatiNEXT,* and the *Latino Book Review.* Ramírez lives with his wife and two children in Sonoma County, California.

CYNDIE RANDALL's poems appear in *minnesota review, DIAGRAM, The Florida Review, Frontier Poetry,* and elsewhere. She works as a therapist in a small town near Lake Michigan. For more, please visit cyndierandall.com.

CAI RODRIGUES-SHERLEY is a poet and educator. A 2020 Pushcart Prize nominee, their work can be found in *Brooklyn Review*, *Crazyhorse*, and *Peach Mag*, among others, as well as *My Loves: A Digital Anthology of Queer Love Poems* from Ghost City Press. His micro-chapbook *MY PARENTS WOULD HAVE NAMED ME SHEFFIELD* is forthcoming with Kissing Dynamite (2023). Cai holds an MFA in creative writing from New York University and lives in Washington, DC, where he works with young writers.

ANNY TANG's poetry appears in the *Literary Review of Canada*, *Room*, *Prairie Fire*, *Arc Poetry Magazine*, and *Grain*. Her work has been shortlisted for the PEN Canada New Voices Award and selected as a Notable Poem in *Best Canadian Poetry*.

BRANDON THURMAN is the author of the chapbook *Strange Flesh* (*Quarterly West*, 2018). A 2021 Gregory Djanikian Scholar, his poetry can be found in *The Adroit Journal*, *Beloit Poetry Journal*, *Nashville Review*, *Sixth Finch*, and others. He lives in the Arkansas Ozarks with his husband and son. You can find him online at brandonthurman.com or on Twitter @bthurman87.

WYETH THOMAS is originally from Salem, Oregon. He is a PhD candidate in English and creative writing at the University of Utah. His most recent work appears in *Western Humanities Review* and *The Gettysburg Review*. He currently lives in Salt Lake City.

KIERON WALQUIST is a queer autistic poet and hillbilly from Missouri. His chapbook, *Love Locks*, was selected by Luther Hughes for the 2022 Quarterly West Chapbook Contest. He holds an MFA in poetry from Washington University in St. Louis and is currently a 2022–2023 FAWC Fellow. Kieron still likes horses and is still healing.

ROSS WHITE is the director of Bull City Press, an independent publisher of poetry, fiction, and nonfiction. He is the author of three chapbooks: *How We Came Upon the Colony*, *The Polite Society*, and *Valley of Want*. His poems have appeared in *American Poetry Review*, *New England Review*, *Ploughshares*, *Poetry Daily*, *Tin House*, and *The Southern Review*, among others. He teaches creative writing and grammar at the University of North Carolina at Chapel Hill and co-hosts *The Chapbook*, a podcast devoted to tiny wonderful things. Follow him on Twitter: @rosswhite.

AVA WINTER's poetry has appeared in *The Baffler*, *Beloit Poetry Journal*, *Four Way Review*, *Grist*, *Meridian*, *Ninth Letter*, *Poetry International*, *TriQuarterly*, and *Tupelo Quarterly*. Their poetry chapbook, *Safe House*, was published by Thrush Press. They are currently pursuing a PhD in creative writing at the University of Nebraska in Lincoln.

ERIC YIP was born and raised in Hong Kong. He was the 2021 winner of the National Poetry Competition in the UK. His work appears in *The Poetry Review*, *The Adroit Journal*, *wildness*, and elsewhere. He is currently an undergraduate at the University of Cambridge.

MARIYA ZILBERMAN is a writer whose poems have recently appeared in *Ploughshares*, *Kenyon Review*, *Columbia Journal*, and *Guesthouse*. She won the 2020 Ploughshares Emerging Writer's Award in Poetry, and has also received support from organizations such as the Vermont Studio Center, the Barbara Deming Memorial Fund, and the New Jewish Culture Fellowship. Mariya was born in Minsk, Belarus, and now lives in Detroit, Michigan. She earned an MFA from the University of Michigan, where she currently teaches. She is at work on her first poetry collection.

Participating Magazines

32 Poems
32poems.com

Able Muse
ablemuse.com

The Account
theaccountmagazine.com

The Adroit Journal
theadroitjournal.org

AGNI
agnionline.bu.edu

Alien Magazine
alienliterarymagazine.com

ANMLY
anmly.org

Apple Valley Review
applevalleyreview.com

ARTS & LETTERS
artsandletters.gcsu.edu

Bat City Review
batcityreview.com

Bayou Magazine
bayoumagazine.org

Beestung
beestungmag.com

Bellevue Literary Review
blreview.org

Beloit Poetry Journal
bpj.org

Bennington Review
benningtonreview.org

Better Than Starbucks
betterthanstarbucks.org

Birmingham Poetry Review
uab.edu/cas/englishpublications/
    birmingham-poetry-review

The Bitter Oleander
bitteroleander.com

Blackbird
blackbird.vcu.edu

Black Warrior Review
bwr.ua.edu

Bloodroot
bloodrootlit.org

Booth: A Journal
booth.butler.edu

Boulevard
boulevardmagazine.org

The Carolina Quarterly
thecarolinaquarterly.com

Carve Magazine
carvezine.com

Cave Wall
cavewallpress.com

Cherry Tree
washcoll.edu/cherrytree

Chestnut Review
chestnutreview.com

Cider Press Review
ciderpressreview.com

Cincinnati Review
cincinnatireview.com

Coal Hill Review
coalhillreview.com

The Rupture
therupturemag.com

Connecticut River Review
ctpoetry.net/connecticut-river-review.html

Copper Nickel
copper-nickel.org

Crazyhorse
crazyhorse.cofc.edu

Cutleaf
cutleafjournal.com

Denver Quarterly
du.edu/denverquarterly

Diode
diodepoetry.com

DIALOGIST
dialogist.org

Ecotone
ecotonemagazine.org

EVENT Magazine
eventmagazine.ca

Fairy Tale Review
fairytalereview.com

The Fiddlehead
thefiddlehead.ca

The Florida Review
floridareview.cah.ucf.edu

Foglifter
foglifterjournal.com

Foothill: A Journal of Poetry
cgu.edu/foothill

The Fourth River
thefourthriver.com

Free State Review
freestatereview.com

The Georgia Review
thegeorgiareview.com

The Gettysburg Review
gettysburgreview.com

Gingerbread House Literary Magazine
gingerbreadhouselitmag.com

Greensboro Review
greensbororeview.org

Guernica
guernicamag.com

Hamilton Arts & Letters
HALmagazine.com

Hayden's Ferry Review
haydensferryreview.com

The Hopkins Review
hopkinsreview.com

After Happy Hour Review
afterhappyhourreview.com

Image
imagejournal.org

Jabberwock Review
jabberwock.org.msstate.edu

Jet Fuel Review
jetfuelreview.com

Kenyon Review
kenyonreview.org

La Presa
embajadoraspress.com

The Lascaux Review
lascauxreview.com

Lucky Jefferson
luckyjefferson.com

The MacGuffin
schoolcraft.edu/macguffin

The Malahat Review
malahatreview.ca

The Margins
aaww.org

Massachusetts Review
massreview.org

Memorious: A Journal of New Verse & Fiction
memorious.org

Mid-American Review
casit.bgsu.edu/midamericanreview

Minola Review
minolareview.com

Minyan Magazine
minyanmag.com

Mississippi Review
www.mississippireview.com

New England Review
nereview.com

Newfound
newfound.org

New Orleans Review
neworleansreview.org

The Night Heron Barks
nightheronbarks.com

Nimrod International Journal
artsandsciences.utulsa.edu/nimrod/

Nurture
nurtureliterary.com

Okay Donkey
okaydonkeymag.com

Pacifica Literary Review
pacificareview.com

PANK
pankmagazine.com

Passages North
passagesnorth.com

Pembroke Magazine
pembrokemagazine.com

Pigeon Pages
pigeonpagesnyc.com

Ploughshares
pshares.org

The Pinch
pinchjournal.com

Poem-A-Day
poets.org/poem-day

Poet Lore
poetlore.com

The Poet's Billow
thepoetsbillow.org

Posit Journal
positjournal.com

Prism Review
sites.laverne.edu/prism-review

Puerto del Sol
puertodelsol.org

Quarterly West
quarterlywest.com

Raleigh Review
RaleighReview.org

Ran Off with the Star Bassoon
ranoffwiththestarbassoon.com

Rat's Ass Review
ratsassreview.net

Roanoke Review
roanokereview.org

Room Magazine
roommagazine.com

Ruminate Magazine
ruminatemagazine.com

Salamander
salamandermag.org

Salt Hill Journal
salthilljournal.net

The Santa Clara Review
santaclarareview.com

Sapiens
sapiens.org

The Seventh Wave
theseventhwave.co

Sewanee Review
thesewaneereview.com

Shenandoah
shenandoahliterary.org

Sine Theta Magazine
sinetheta.net

Slab
slablitmag.org

SLICE Magazine
slicemagazine.org

Slippery Elm
slipperyelm.findlay.edu

The Southeast Review
southeastreview.org

The Southern Review
thesouthernreview.org

Split Lip Magazine
splitlipthemag.com

storySouth
storysouth.com

Sugar House Review
SugarHouseReview.com

Sundog Lit
sundoglit.com

SWWIM Every Day
swwim.org

Tahoma Literary Review
tahomaliteraryreview.com

Terrain
terrain.org

Thrush Poetry Journal
thrushpoetryjournal.com

Tinderbox Poetry Journal
tinderboxpoetry.com

upstreet
upstreet-mag.org

Up the Staircase Quarterly
upthestaircase.org

Virginia Quarterly Review
vqronline.org

Washington Square Review
washingtonsquarereview.com

Whale Road Review
whaleroadreview.com

wildness
readwildness.com

Willow Springs
willowspringsmagazine.org

The Yale Review
yalereview.org

ZYZZYVA
zyzzyva.org

Participating Programs

Chatham University MFA in Creative Writing
chatham.edu/mfa

Florida International University MFA in Creative Writing
english.fiu.edu/creative-writing

Hollins University Jackson Center for Creative Writing
hollinsmfa.wordpress.com

Johns Hopkins The Writing Seminars
writingseminars.jhu.edu

Kansas State University MFA in Creative Writing Program
k-state.edu/english/programs/cw

McNeese State University MFA Program
mfa.mcneese.edu

Minnesota State University Mankato Creative Writing Program
english.mnsu.edu/cw

Monmouth University Creative Writing
monmouth.edu/school-of-humanities-social-sciences/ma-english.aspx

New Mexico State University MFA in Creative Writing
english.nmsu.edu/graduate-programs/mfa

New School Writing Program
newschool.edu/writing

New York University Creative Writing Program
as.nyu.edu/cwp

Northwestern University MA/MFA in Creative Writing
sps.northwestern.edu/program-areas/graduate/creative-writing

The Ohio State University MFA Program in Creative Writing
english.osu.edu/mfa

Ohio University Creative Writing PhD
ohio.edu/cas/english/grad/creative-writing/index.cfm

San Diego State University MFA in Creative Writing
mfa.sdsu.edu

Southeast Missouri State University Master of Arts in English
semo.edu/english

Stony Brook Southampton MFA in Creative Writing
stonybrook.edu/southampton/mfa/cwl

Syracuse University MFA in Creative Writing
english.syr.edu/cw/cw-program.html

Texas Tech University Creative Writing Program
depts.ttu.edu/english/cw

UMass Amherst MFA for Poets and Writers
umass.edu/englishmfa

UMass Boston MFA Program in Creative Writing
umb.edu/academics/cla/english/grad/mfa

UNC Greensboro Creative Writing Program
mfagreensboro.org

University of Alabama at Birmingham Graduate Theme in Creative Writing
uab.edu/cas/english/graduate-program/creative-writing

University of Connecticut Creative Writing Program
creativewriting.uconn.edu

University of Idaho MFA in Creative Writing
uidaho.edu/class/english/graduate/mfa-creative-writing

University of Illinois at Chicago Program for Writers
engl.uic.edu/CW

University of Kansas Graduate Creative Writing Program
englishcw.ku.edu

University of Mississippi MFA in Creative Writing
mfaenglish.olemiss.edu

University of New Orleans Creative Writing Workshop
uno.edu/writing

University of North Texas Creative Writing
english.unt.edu/creative-writing-0

University of San Francisco MFA in Writing
usfca.edu/mfa

University of Southern Mississippi Center for Writers
usm.edi/writers

University of Texas Michener Center for Writers
michener.utexas.edu

University of Utah Creative Writing Program
english.utah.edu

University of South Florida Creative Writing
english.usf.edu/graduate/concentrations/cw/degrees/

Virginia Tech MFA in Creative Writing Program
liberalarts.vt.edu/departments-and-schools/department-of-english/academic-programs/master-of-fine-arts-
   in-creative-writing.html

Western Michigan University Creative Writing Program
wmich.edu/english

West Virginia University MFA Program
creativewriting.wvu.edu

The series editor wishes to thank the many poets involved in our first round of reading:

Hodges Adams, Kate Coleman, Katherine James, Kyle Marbut, Jeddie Sophronius, and Raisa Tolchinsky

Special thanks to Jason Coleman and the University of Virginia Press for editorial advice and support, and to John Barnett of 4 Eyes Design for his cover magic.